RELIGIOUS ART IN
THE TWENTIETH CENTURY

RELIGIOUS ART IN THE TWENTIETH CENTURY

PIE-RAYMOND RÉGAMEY

HERDER AND HERDER

1963
HERDER AND HERDER   NEW YORK
232 Madison Avenue, New York 16, N.Y.

English language adaptation of *Art sacré au XXe siècle?*
Paris, Editions du Cerf, 1952.

Nihil obstat: Edward J. Sutfin, Ph.D.
             Censor librorum
Imprimatur: † Robert F. Joyce
            Bishop of Burlington
            July 3, 1963

CONTENTS

INTRODUCTION

When fifteen years ago I and my associates in the editing of *Journal of Arts and Letters* introduced Father Régamey's studies to the English-speaking Catholic community, we had little idea of the true scope of his work or of the revolutionary impact it would have on Catholic sensibility. Since that time, Father Régamey has become more and more widely known and esteemed by the publication of some of his writings on the spiritual life, and by the translation of a number of other essays on art criticism. This decade has been a period of transition during which the work of a few pioneering theorists and artists—such as Maurice Lavanoux, Walter Shewring, H. A. Reinhold, Ann Grill, Sister Thomasita, Frank Kacmarcik, Sister Mary of the Compassion, Barry Byrne, and many other equally divergent figures—has been consolidated, so that these defenders of a contemporary idiom no longer sound like voices from the underground, and so that Catholics in general no longer feel they must develop apologetic squints when faced with a modern work. It is due in great part to the efforts of Fathers Régamey and Couturier that Catholics in America and England, and, of course, on the continent as well, are now able to accept openly what had previously been decried as "untraditional"—a word, as Kilian McDonnell noted in

Worship's important art symposium of five years ago, which has been much abused by defenders of the *status quo*.

It is commonly realized, as it was not a decade and a half ago, that we are experiencing in our time a development of art forms which have many of the characteristics of the sacred art of the past: these forms are often non-representational, non-rational though highly intellectual, hieratic, and abstract. If the enumeration of these qualities seems to place an unwarranted emphasis on the negative, this is not surprising; for, the sacred is to be defined to a great extent by its sense of separation and segregation, since it shares not only in the affirmative way of religious philosophers, but in the *via negativa* of the mystics.

Yet, paradoxically, this art of our time with all its sacral traits often remains an art dedicated to the exploitation of the world of the profane, of that world beyond the wall of the temple. And it is the resulting conflict within the artist, responsive to an innate passion for the sacred while orienting his work towards profane ends, that accounts perhaps both for the frustration and the agony embodied in much contemporary work which seems tormented by a kind of schizoid malaise, and also for the hesitant and almost covert manner in which the great exponents of sacred forms —one thinks of Picasso, Masson, or even of Pollock—introduce the images of the world of spirit, of the world of the temple into their art; moreover, while shunning the notion of an infinite absolute, these artists often seem to strive after a sort of impossible numerical infinity in the incessant repetition of themes and figures drawn from the realm of the myth. They appear, in fact, haunted by the sacred, while tormented by their inability to embrace an absolute which would allow complete freedom to this holy daimon within them.

Considering, then, this sacral character in modern art, though without ignoring its apparent dedication to profane ends, one may feel justified in anticipating for our age a renaissance without historic parallel of all the religious arts. The expectation of this renewal in these arts—that is, of the arts employing the traditional language of the sacred, and directed towards the work of the temple—is based not merely on the assumption that modern man, as eminent thinkers have reminded us, is in search of a soul, but rather on that necessary metaphysical law which states that a number of accidental mutations predisposes to substantial change.

Given the gradual purification of the arts beginning with the romantic rebellion against the academy, progressing through the achievement of Cézanne in rejecting mere sensation in his vision of a deeper architectural form, up to the astringently purgative experiments of the revolutionary artists of this century, it is manifest that the twilight and the dark night of the absolute have faded into a new dawn. One might further suggest that the absence of this sense of the absolute from the art of the last three centuries represents a type of spiritual vastation, similar to that of which the mystics have written, and that the lustral mission of Cézanne and his sucessors has constituted a saving ascesis for the modern sensibility; and it is through this asceticism that the prince of darkness, the tutelary spirit of Malraux' twilight, has been exorcised.

Now, it is the great merit of Father Régamey's book that it displays both great sympathy for the plight of contemporary artists and that breadth of theological understanding which is necessary to justify their entrance into the field of liturgical art. This justification may perhaps be best illustrated on the basis that any art work, whether by pagan or Christian, remains a natural thing functioning in a manner similar to the natural theology of Aristotle in relation to the Christian theology of Aquinas: it leads one to the foot of the altar; it does not, nor is it intended that it should, bring about a communion with the Presence there. Even in the case of an artist assumed to be "atheist," there is no justification for excluding his work from the church on religious grounds—though prudence might suggest reasons—for the art work is likened to a sacramental rather than to a sacrament: that is, it takes its Christian character not from the mere fact of its being "confected" and directed by the artist to liturgical ends, but from the prayer of the whole Mystical Body to whose service it is ordained when it is blessed or consecrated with the church building.

Father Régamey, as I have noted above, does acknowledge that not every artist merely by achieving a work of some excellence has a *de facto* right to employ his talents in a liturgical art. For, prescinding from the ordinary exercise of critical intelligence, there are examples of condemnations of contemporary work which are in every way justifiable, and which may even be said to serve the cause of artistic progress. These are the expressions of the bishops when it is a matter of safeguarding for prudential and doctrinal reasons the faithful of their own dioceses against the occasional shocks which the distortion or the novelty of certain works may cause. No one, of course, would claim that bishops are more highly endowed esthetically than the rest of mankind, but in virtue of their office, of their experience, and of their empathic awareness of the condition of the faithful, they have a right and a duty to interdict whatever may disturb their people unnecessarily. Moreover, such interdiction will have over the years the beneficial result of obviating the danger of any extended reaction setting in permanently against the contemporary art forms.

Thus, the removal of Richier's crucifix from the chapel at Assy—to take a notable example of episcopal supervision —could be justified on prudential and doctrinal grounds, not on esthetic. Nevertheless the obligation of making a valid judgment in such cases demands that each art work be assessed individually, so that what may be considered imprudent in one diocese might be acceptable in another; and what would offend insular parochial standards might be a stimulus to reverent prayer in the clearer atmosphere of a university or monastic community.

Condemnations such as that of the Richier sculpture point up another area where Father Régamey has introduced some necessary clarifications: to what extent is the artist justified in distorting the body of Christ to conform to his own creative intuition? This problem, which seems to vex unduly those who never before took an interest in the religious arts, can be resolved only by an examination of the entire continuum of Christian art. Down through the centuries every artist has portrayed the God-man according to the dictates of his own inspiration, yet it is obvious that the Christ of the catacombs differs from the Christ of Giotto, of Michelangelo, of El Greco, or of Rouault. As this book suggests, the artist is not to be regarded as an experimenter who is using the body of Christ merely as a pretext for exploring new forms in a technical exercise, but rather he is to be seen as an imitator of the *supremus Artifex* who formed in the womb of the Virgin the body of the Son of God. Each artist's representation, then, is an attempt to "utter the good Word" in a necessarily fragmentary and partial approximation of the heights and depths in Him who was described as a worm and no man, and also as the most beautiful of the sons of man.

We are concerned in this problem with artistic objectives only; for, if the form given to the body of Christ—whether it be the religious oleograph or the so-called Jansenist crucifix—has been guided exclusively by religious principles, it will be defective not by reason of any possibly erroneous dogmatic conception, but by reason of its derivation from non-esthetic sources. Similarly, a pure work generated in the purest interiority, but judged unfit for liturgical use on prudential or doctrinal bases, generally ought not to be modified to make it acceptable, for once the integrity of the original esthetic impulse is tampered with, the way is open to continuing abuse. And, historically, it will often be found that the artist, depending on his own sensibility and artistic vision, has grasped the doctrinal significance more firmly than his critics who do not really see his work, and so reject it in the name of a spurious theological accuracy. The artist must, of course, rely on theological wisdom, but such a reliance should not be founded on an abstract knowledge of the Christian fact and its corollaries, since then the Christianity of the work will be constituted as merely an artificial and appliqué element. Instead there should be a gradual and organic assimilation of this theological wisdom so that it will be molded into the form of the work from the very moment of its inception.

The last point which I would emphasize here, and upon which Father Régamey's book casts some necessary light, is the affirmation that there is no such thing as a "liturgical style." Neither the pure and firmly delicate elongations of Eric Gill nor the earth-slung forms of Jean Charlot—who has rightly accused some of Gill's followers of mannerism—can lay claim to being the "approved" idiom for an ecclesiastical art. In the renaissance of the religious arts which we are now experiencing, and towards which Father Régamey's writings have been a significant contribution, all styles as all men have a voice in singing the new canticle. And though each artist shall sing in his own tongue, all shall be understood in the one language of the arts celebrating the magnalia Dei.

At the conclusion of an address delivered before the Congress for the Reconstruction of Churches (Rotterdam, May, 1948), Father Régamey declared: "I want to remark, through gratitude, that this doctrine is only an application to the case you have submitted to me of some formulae which Jacques Maritain drew up in 1920." So, too, it has been my task in this brief introduction to extend that tradition of gratitude by attempting to point out the relevance of the present work to the English-speaking world.

JUSTUS GEORGE LAWLER

PART I

THE DEMANDS AND IDEALS
OF SACRED ART

1

The Problem of Christian Art

The fine arts are truly in conformity with religion when, "like noble handmaids, they enter the service of divine worship." These words of Pius XI, echoed later by Pius XII,[1] must be understood in their deepest sense. Considered superficially, the liturgy appears to be composed of rites and words. But in fact it is the celebration of the Christian mystery in time, the mystery, hidden before all time, even from the angels, now revealed to the elect.[2] It is the reunion of all things in Christ, whether in heaven or on earth.[3] In other words, the liturgy is the accomplishment in time of Christ's eternal priesthood. In the heights of heaven, Christ is interceding for us endlessly.[4] He is forever the sacrificed Lamb,[5] and his offering gives life to all mankind. He has given us the means of offering this same sacrifice, celebrating this same mystery—and that is the liturgy. For this the Church was made, being the completion of him who everywhere

---

[1] From the encyclical *Mediator Dei*, November 20, 1947.
[2] Eph. 3:9, Col. 1:26.
[3] Eph. 1:10.
[4] Heb. 7:25.
[5] Apoc. 5:6–14.

and in all things is complete.[6] This completion is often
cloaked in appearances of the least significant things. The
more powerfully the eternal mystery works through time,
the more fitting it seems that its working should be detached from the temporal. Thus we can be made to see
beyond what is seen—brief words, some bread and wine, a
little water, a touch of oil for anointing, or a hand out-
stretched over the head of someone who will thereafter be
a priest for all eternity. We are made with an imagination,
and images are to help us into a sphere where images are no
longer needed.

Ceremonies thus have the function of enacting mystery
in the form of symbols, thereby expressing its every aspect.
The liturgy is even more than the height of religious art, the
primary or major sacred art. In their externals, ceremonies
are art, but their invisible substance is precisely the substance of those things we hope for, and the beginning of
things unseen.[7] Those words are a definition of faith, but
they apply equally well to the liturgical mysteries which
medieval theologians called the "sacraments of faith." The
substance of the things we hope for acts within us in the
measure in which we believe. Our faith needs to be aroused,
supported, and guided; it must be given a favorable atmosphere to which our whole being contributes, for its development. All of this is what the living ceremonies of religion
are meant to do. Against the Protestants, the Council of
Trent declared that the function of ceremonial is to "rouse
up the minds of the faithful to contemplate the sublime

[6] Eph. 1:23.
[7] Heb. 11:1.

realities hidden in the sacrifice of the mass."[8] In turn, the ceremonies are reflected in the architecture of the churches in which they are celebrated; in the decoration of the churches, which explains in imagery the things that take place in the liturgy; and in the music, which opens the soul to the worship of God. In every case, the art that Christianity uses is meant to contribute something to the mystery which the Church celebrates to bring it to perfection and fulfillment.

Ceremonies, rites, and texts are not influenced by the contingencies of time so greatly as are architecture, paintting, sculpture, and music—the "minor arts"—which are subservient to the major art of the liturgy. It is their function to act as links between the liturgy and the changing pattern of space and time. They must needs be affected by the marks of time. Whatever permanent and unchanging demands faith may make of them, they will always take the form of concrete and contemporary manifestations, involved in a particular place and time. There are timeless rules for religious art, but as soon as we try to put them into effect, faith itself, the longing for eternity, brings us down to the here and now.

The twentieth century is an age of revolution. Such changes have occurred and are occurring in our ways of thinking, feeling, seeing, and living that even the most confirmed traditionalists are obliged to formulate artistic data in a way that is completely different from and at times even opposed to the formulations of the past. This applies to nothing so much as to the whole question of the Church's

[8] Council of Trent, Sess. 22, chap. 5 (Denzinger 1746 [943]).

position in the present-day world, and it explains why the demands which the faith makes of art today—demands on the artist, the faithful, and the clergy—are caught up in a tangle of uncertainties.

The sharpest example of the problem occurs when we consider the function of religious art in relation to the secular world. A typical example is the church which was built at Boendael in the suburbs of Brussels in 1945, Saint-Adrien. It was enormous, and entirely out of proportion with the little houses surrounding it. The reason given for building this vast edifice was that tall apartment buildings were to be erected in that area. Thus it was decided that the church should dominate the whole area from the start. But today's resources no longer allow such a vast structure to be erected with integrity. Immensity was achieved by all sorts of obviously unsatisfactory means that made the building look as improbable as a piece of stage architecture. The only message it conveyed was that the church was laying pretentious claims to a place in the life of the city which its actual state and its true conditions could not in fact justify. In other words, it was a pathetic sham.

When we are brought fact to face with the problem in such a way, we have to admit at the outset that modern civilization does not allow the Church the place she has always considered her own. The Church stands by her rights and by her ideals, which are symbolized in the Gospel image of the hen gathering her chicks under her wings. She must no longer seem to play a role which is not really her own. She must content herself with the space proportionate to her congregations and to the resources at her disposal for truly honest construction of her buildings. She requires architects to take account of her dignity without ostentation or vanity. The Church of the Gospel, filled as she is by the Holy Spirit, counts on the spiritual quality of the arts. She will no longer impose herself, she will radiate light and warmth.

The architect Émile Steffann, meditating on the ruins of Cologne, reminded us that we must never conceive of God's house as anything but a tent set up on the journey to eternity, a place of temporary refuge.[9] Meistermann, the maker of stained-glass windows, regarded the destroying fire from heaven as having been sent by Truth, and wondered whether we had the right to set up these ruins again before laying the foundation anew.[10]

Yet against these views it must be said that the work of man's hands cannot be limited to expressing what man is in this day and age. Man's buildings are models for his growth, the blueprint of what he must become. He will erect his churches as worthy symbols of what God should be for him. He will not let these churches stand as signs of his disavowal. It has long been argued whether the churches we are building are to reveal the place that belongs to Christ in the modern world or the humble position which an age of unbelief has assigned to him.

To resolve the problem, we might remember the sacri-

[9] From a letter quoted in L'Art Sacré, November–December, 1950.

[10] Cited in Kirchen in Trümmern, published for the seventh centenary of the Cathedral of Cologne (Cologne: Balduin Pick Verlag, 1948).

fices of Christian communities for their churches. The ancient cathedrals in their vastness and beauty were the works
of men whose standing seems to us of the very lowest kind.
They denied themselves so that they might put up these
monuments. We have no right to them any longer, because
we are not prepared to go without our comforts, our amuse-
ments. We are not necessarily wrong if we fail to give up
these things, but the fact remains that if we do not, we cannot honestly presume to put up buildings of worth and
beauty since the spiritual values that underlie them no
longer matter so much in our lives as we should like to pre-
tend. It is true that the spirit of evangelical simplicity has
a long way to go before it finds a form that will suit our
time, but whatever its form, that spirit will oblige us to
revise our habitual conception of a church, its height, extension, appearance, and decoration.

A church cannot possibly hope materially to compete
with the secular buildings that are going up in our time, let
alone surpass them. The dominating position of a church
has never been justified except in the measure that the
earthly city conceived of itself as a sacred entity. Something
of this kind remains true even today in some Christian
countries, where churches can retain their exceptional proportions, but even then they must differ from other buildings only by the nobility of their form and the great care
taken to make their structure durable. In times past God's
house was simply a transfiguration of the forms and proportions of the houses of his children; there was no separation
between his house and theirs, for Christianity was a living
unity. It was only when that unity was attacked and when

the Church began to be driven back in all spheres that the clergy began to erect those aggressive, authoritarian monuments which, by their very ostentation, indicated the inherent weakness which so much architectural display was meant to camouflage.[11]

But how, in effect, can the Church signify that she is on earth as a spiritual society, and more specifically, to what degree should churches be different from other buildings? It is only in the last hundred years that churches have come to differ systematically from other buildings. When approaching any old Flemish town, you cannot possibly tell from a distance which among all the towers in sight is the church tower, which is the high roof of the market and which the church roof. In Arezzo recently I came across an imposing arcaded façade and a high tower, and it was not until I reached the door that I could recognize it as the parish church of Saint Mary and not the Pretorio. It is a masterpiece of Italian Romanesque, that essentially sacred style. But if you think of any church built during the last hundred years, you will have to admit that it screams a mile off that it is a church and could be nothing else. Whether they be pseudo-Gothic or pretentiously "modern," in all cases these churches seem self-conscious and pathetic, like the pious mannerisms of the overdevout and the unctious tone of voice adopted by some preachers.

It may be argued that sacred things must necessarily be separated from profane, particularly in our time, when the world is so thoroughly paganized. It is not surprising that in the age of faith the church building was an essential part of

[11] Père Couturier, in *L'Art Sacré*, July, 1950, p. 4.

the town, since the whole town bore marks of a religious outlook. But surely, it is said, religious art in our time should take as its first objective an emphasis on the cleavage between the church and the world; otherwise it will become infected by materialism. The answer to this difficulty ought to be primarily a functional one. If the arts honestly fulfill the functional needs of a church—and a church's function is mainly liturgical—then they are likely to produce a building that will look sacred. What is needed is insight, a kind of tact in the handling of forms, which will emerge spontaneously from the sense of the sacred which must animate the artist in his work. As to the danger of profanation—and each age has its own—this disquieting question will recur throughout Part II, where I will discuss the arts of today.

What we must now examine is the relationship which should exist between Christ's Church and human society, for that will also determine the relationship between the church building and the city or village. The Church is catholic, which means universal. Her task is to restore all things in Christ. At the same time, she is also the ark in which the few chosen souls are saved from the flood. Which of these two faces is she to present to the world? Must she try to be as much as possible like the world, since her task is to integrate everything into a synthesis, or must she look away from the world, since she must protect herself from its evil and perdition?

The answer to this question lies in the two definitions of world. If by the world we mean, like St. John, the reign of sin, the Church has nothing in common with the world.

But if we understand the world as God's creation, then it obviously is the Church's concern. The dividing line is invisible. Only God can see what is and what is not of his Church. Sin has touched everything, and yet there is nothing that exists that could not, by the grace of God, become baptizable. But what is of the world is ambivalent, spells salvation or corruption, depending on what use is made of it. That the world in St. John's sense has also encroached upon the Church must not be forgotten. When we are tempted to expect from the Church an expression distinguishing her from the world, let us be wary of the misunderstandings which would cement into that expression some of the tares which the world has scattered in the Church.

On the face of it, one might expect that this same Church, particularized as she appears among human societies, should be given some specific and immediately recognizable form by the arts. But in fact the so-called laws of sacred art, which I shall discuss later, require nothing of the kind. In our day, the Church has a much greater sense of her catholicity, her openness, and her status as the invisible Church made visible. She is being stripped of everything that could give her the appearance of a sect, even a very large sect. She wishes to be recognized as a vital center in which the most diverse human values can find their fullness. Far from freezing the Church's visage under the guise of hierarchism, the sacred arts should make it recognizable, fashion it through the power of the very inspirations which animate Christians. They will be diversified to extremes, according to the places and times; and these variations of Christian art, throughout history and the Church's lands, already so suspect, will be still greater today owing to the more divergent tendencies among men. Even the etymology of the word church tells us that it is an assembly into which all men are called. Like holy Wisdom, which the Church incarnates, she calls out to men in the public places.[12] She calls upon them to transcend the things of this earth, but she calls them nonetheless in the language of men. The arts are false to her if they create the impression that she is an outdated institution or that she belongs to one social class alone or that in order to enter her fold some kind of artificial personality is required.

The arts run the double danger of becoming organs of publicity or mouthpieces of pious conformism. Their aim should be to reach the "naturally Christian soul" in every man, and to tell him that he is not without God in this world,[13] that Christ has come, and that he gives life to all.[14] The arts will give tangible expression to the beatitudes of the Gospel. They will launch an appeal to enter the Church, but not as if it were a matter of entering a public meeting or a show. Coming into the Church leads us to finding our way into the core of our own souls and into the midst of the Christian brotherhood; both are revealed in the depths of God's love. Thus the Church on earth is that place where men reach their own truth by overcoming themselves in God and in their fellow men. She is the center of a contagious fervor that is to win the whole world. The Church is not a propaganda bureau; she is a fellowship, bestowing

[12] Prov. 1:21.
[13] Eph. 2:12.
[14] John 5:21.

on her members the experience of divine love which those outside her communion will see as irresistibly convincing. That is the appeal of the Church on Earth.

It goes without saying that the means of the arts are pitifully inadequate for this mission, but more tragically, the faithful and the clergy themselves are often not aware of what their role is in the city of God on earth. In certain places we do find that true Christian zeal and generosity have made the community spirit live, but zeal is not enough; man lacks imagination, and needs charity to explain sacred meanings. If we could only restore Christian charity to its proper place in people's lives, the whole outlook of religious art would be transformed. We would have no more ostentation, for Christians would realize that at a time when there are men living in less than human conditions, when many churches have fallen into ruin and others are needed but cannot be built for lack of resources, it is scandalous to undertake costly and extravagant projects for the "greater glory of God."

Our Lord's reminder that we would always have the poor among us[15] is seriously misunderstood. It does not mean that poverty is a structural law of society which Our Lord would approve of or regard as providential; his words should not encourage us to take from the poor what is their due for the benefit of luxurious worship. On the contrary, Our Lord taught his disciples that the poor come first in every work of mercy. Their very existence among us must always cause us concern. To demonstrate God's transcendence and the sovereignty of his right even over the law of charity, a cer-

---

[15] Matt. 26:11.

tain profusion is always required in sacred cults—silken
vestments, chalices with gilded bowls—but the whole point
is that this should be poor men's luxury. Everything sacred
is part of the order of charity. Mercy is better than sacrifice.[16] And our religious art can only flourish when the
Christian community can face up to these problems and
become a real assembly of brothers, granting first place to
the poor and to spiritual values and giving the church some
external form that will be true to her reality, drawing the
spiritually minded toward her instead of repelling them.

Our age is concerned not merely with the Church in her
relation to the world but also with her works; unlike the
previous age, ours regards her functions rather than her appearances. There is a renewal of the Church's more ancient
and lasting traditions. Too many people still think that
religious requirements impose a pattern, and one pattern
alone. They have some notion of what a church ought to
look like, and this they adapt more or less suitably to the
requirements of worship. Yet the opposite should obviously
be done—it is the communal liturgical worship to be celebrated in a given place that determines the church's size and
even to an extent its appearance, in the same way that a
shellfish builds his shell. The needs of religion are primarily
the needs of celebration. The sacred character must impose
no historical style nor particular material forms nor allegedly
"religious" conventional details. As the Protestant minister

[16] Osee 6:6, quoted with emphasis by Our Lord (Matt. 9:13,
12:7).

Eckly of Strasbourg put it, the Christian church building is "like a materialization of its inner principle."[17]

What is this principle? When the functions of a church are discussed nowadays in order to establish its architectural form, two conceptions are often set in opposition: is the church primarily the house of God or primarily the gathering place of the faithful? The liturgy of the dedication of a church, as some liturgists will tell us,[18] puts the emphasis on the former. On the other hand, as Martimort suggests, if an architect designs a church which resembles a movie theater or a stadium, there is nothing here to which a liturgist can take exception, since this was the usage of the fourth century when church assemblies took place in palaces and baths.[19] Thus we are presented with two types of church, one reaching heavenward, full of mystery, with a vast sanctuary, the full participation of the faithful being only a secondary consideration, and the other type with the accent on people and community, where good visibility has been the chief consideration, with the sanctuary being more or less lost in a vast auditorium. Each of these types represents a valid principle, but it should be quite possible to combine the two.

If we begin with the idea of God's house, for all practical purposes we will soon arrive at the idea of a house of the faithful. For if God's being were exclusively confined to the

[17] *Essai sur l'Architecture religieuse en fonction de la Communauté chrétienne de son Culte*, thesis submitted at the School of Protestant Theology, University of Strasbourg, typescript.

[18] A. M. Roguet, "*Qu'est-ce qu'une Église?*" *Cahiers de L'Art Sacré*, no. 1 (1945).

[19] Canon Martimort, in *ibid.*, p. 30.

depths of his infinite mystery, he would need no houses of
any sort here below. It is because he is living among us, because of us, in fact, that he sets up his tent among men. The
most theocentric type of Christian worship we could possibly imagine is still always for man. God's "accidental" glory,
as the theologians call it, is in the sanctification of man.[20]
The mass is our banquet, the sacraments are for our benefit
—propter homines. If on the other hand we begin with the
idea of the Christian community, it is perfectly obvious that
we have to think immediately in terms of the altar and
sanctuary, for the community only comes into being through
the celebration of the eucharist. Christ's Mystical Body is
this assembly of the faithful, whose whole reason for as-
sembling is their common participation in Christ in the
eucharist.

Therefore it would seem more appropriate if instead of
concentrating on either the sanctuary or the place for the
congregation we aimed at some living fusion of the two. But
they remain distinct and must not be confused. Though
they are housed under the same roof, the sanctuary must be
seen to be a still more sacred place than the remaining space
of the sacred building. The liturgy can be envisaged as being
celebrated in the center of the community and radiating in
all directions,[21] or it can be thought of as a procession leading from baptistry to altar, from the present time to the
second coming. But in either case, the altar will be the
spiritual center of the whole conception.

[20] Summa Theologiae, II, II, q. 132, art. 1, ad 2.
[21] A radiating plan, but not necessarily a polygon with the altar in
the center. The question has been much debated.

Participation in the eucharist is a very different thing from attendance at a spectacle. However gripping a profane performance may be, however closely it knits the watchers in the audience, it can never be on the same level as the eucharistic assembly of Christians as brothers. The link between spectators is merely accidental. They are all in front of the show, watching what is going on. For this reason alone, it would seem impractical to build churches after the fashion of movie theaters and stadiums, for instance, with tiers of seats.

In the past, the faithful appear to have been satisfied with following the liturgy at some distance, often separated from the altar by a screen which put the whole celebration out of the sight of those present. Nowadays, the faithful are aware that something much more interesting—an active participation in the liturgy—is available to them. The church in which this full share in the liturgy is possible needs to be conceived in this new light, particularly since modern building techniques have created new possibilities. Broader roof space can be so balanced as to require no supports that impede the view of the congregation, and this implies completely new lines and shapes in the church in place of those with which we are familiar and to which we are often sentimentally too attached. Instead of producing pastiches of traditional forms which are beyond our means, we need new structures, new forms.

There is nothing that need be shocking to a true sense of religion in adopting modern techniques and the new forms they offer us, since our first task is to face facts and to think in terms of community functions and how they are best performed. We should discard any sense of sentimental obligation to the past with its Gothic arches and its spires. These forms, however much we covet them, cannot in our day be genuine, true, or pure.

The need to face facts, to be honest about requirements and functions, is the only fundamental determinant for the things we use in our Christian worship. Granted that some sacred, mysterious character must be retained in the church building, when it comes to the vessels and objects used in the mass, the only standard is their use. Here again, the past has familiarized us with many forms, and their study is very useful. Take, for instance, the ciborium. If the lip of the ciborium is curved slightly inward, the priest can be sure that no hosts will fall out. This is important, as it is that the stem of the ciborium be easy to hold, with no decoration likely to hurt the fingers holding it; quite subordinate to the main consideration of its use is the ciborium's symbolic ornamentation. Symbols can be favorable aids to devotion, but if they are not discreet and simple in meaning and composition, they can be intolerable.

Symbolic decoration has been dreadfully abused. There is something so perfect and pure about undecorated linen that embroidered crosses and emblems and crowns of thorns should be avoided as a woeful distraction to the priest saying mass, if not as ugly pretensions, which they often are. But we are unfortunately still hidebound by a long inheritance of redundant and misguided symbolism. Durandus of Mende, for instance, in his *Rationale* even went so far as to discover special significance in candles, wax, wick, and flame. Such finicky late-medieval irrelevance is worlds removed from true symbolism as it was understood in the early Christian period.[22] Many people consider a chasuble to be insufficiently sacred if it bears no traditional symbols, especially a cross on the back; some think that the Y-shaped orphrey is a cross. In reality, the Church has no such requirements. The true symbolism of vestments lies simply in their six liturgical colors and in the fact that the vestment itself stands for the charity of Christ in which the priest is clothed. In use, the chasuble reveals its significance clearly enough without any pedantry added to serve as a catechism lesson. The simple beauty of the vestment is all that the mind needs from this particular object to help it in the contemplation of the mysteries of the mass.

The early Fathers of the Church and medieval writers are agreed that church decoration serves to instruct the untutored. Walafrid Strabo even considered painting to be the literature of the uneducated. This outlook is no longer justified. Should we conclude, then, that the days of religious paintings are gone, since today nearly all the faithful are able to read? Furthermore, as early as the ninth century, St. Nicephorus was suggesting a somewhat more psychological reason for church decoration, one which would apply to all men, educated or not: visual representations have more power over the imagination than the written or spoken word. But even this theory no longer justifies the use of decorations of an instructive kind today. Movies, television, and illustrated magazines affect the imagination in a way quite different from the paintings and sculptures of our

[22] Roguet, op. cit.

churches. We can count on them no longer for similar effects; they have to some extent been relieved of their power.
We may indeed ask ourselves not only how much the faithful would see of each bas-relief at Chartres, for instance, but
how much they would in fact understand. The kings of
Judea on the façade of the Cathedral of Notre Dame eventually came to be thought the kings of France.

And even when images are recognizable, we must be care-
ful not to exaggerate their evocative value. If they are bad,
they can be esthetically intolerable. And how good are they,
in fact, as instruments for instructing the faithful? One sus-
pects that their lesson can be as fleeting as that of the coffin
which some seventeenth-century pope had made at his
coronation to keep in his room before his eyes so that he
would be able to avoid the sin of nepotism. His nephew,
they say, was made a cardinal in less time than it takes to
tell! Villon's mother was impressed by the "painted paradise of harps and lutes" and the corresponding hell where
the damned were boiled, but we also know that the Ceme-
tery of the Innocents with its terrible *Danse Macabre* was
a trafficking ground for prostitutes, a rendezvous for gay
parties and high society.

In fact, religious painting would seem to have little lasting
influence on the thought and the will of Christians. It is
enough to note the outrages the public tolerates against
some of the most impressive works of art to doubt whether
they have the edifying effect that they should. Not too
much should be expected from the sacred arts. The profane
notion expressed both by the German Romantics and by
Kierkegaard that artistic creation is of the "ironic" order

applies to the spectator as well as to the creator. Bossuet
feared that passionate actions witnessed on the stage were
bound to have an evil influence on people's lives, but as
Père Deman has well observed, these actions are not really
lived by the spectators who are only "in a state of comedy."
This "ironic" character of images in relation to life has
today increased to such an extent that we might almost
speak of their demise.

It is in particular the representation of the things of faith
that to modern men seems unreal and incredible. We shall
not easily disabuse them of this view. It will remain the task
of the arts to remind us constantly of some of the most
central supernatural realities. Their representations will
continue to be the theme of sermons from the pulpit, but
it is evident that the so-called mute preaching of works of
art in churches is no longer heard with the required simplicity. Many of the arguments of former ages, therefore,
lead to conclusions contrary to those which our ancestors
were entitled to draw.

The artist today has above all to create an atmosphere
favorable for a worthy celebration of the liturgy. This comes
before any artistic catechising, whether we are thinking of
the needs of the faithful or of the possibilities of the arts
themselves. Nevertheless, church decoration will always
have an element of the didactic. Decoration will always
profit by the use of some of the great traditional themes of
Christian art, because man himself will always profit by the
sight and remembrance of the figures and major themes
which make tangible the fundamental realities by which
he must live. It will also be a help to the preacher, whose

message will be amplified by visible illustrations of his
subjects. Long after his words have faded into silence, the
image can recall in some measure the message he brings
to us.

But as regards actual instruction, painting in churches
should always be restrained. It will not be the more instructive for treating of a multitude of things. It often seems as
though the churches built in our own time require people
to learn a host of irrelevant things before they can be
Christians. The usual encumbrance of our churches with
all kinds of statues suggests that Christianity is a hodge-
podge of childishness, legend, and misplaced devotion.[23]

Père Roguet has reminded us that in church decoration,
order and evaluation are more instructive than a detailed
visual rendition of articles of faith. A preacher should never
speak about any one point of theology without having at the
back of his mind a unified scheme of the whole of theology.
Similarly, what is needed in a church is a good large nave
and a simple altar visibly dominated by the crucifix. Devotions, with their statues, should not be suppressed but
relegated to the side chapels. The mystery of the cross
and the altar is at the heart of Christian worship, and everything else is secondary, optional, which does not mean that
it is unimportant. A church cannot be decorated by ac-
cumulating artistic details, however pleasant and edifying
they may be. It must be considered as the doctrinal whole,
which the decorations should serve to fix in the minds
of the faithful. All too often, when we go into a church, we

[23] A. M. Roguet, "Pour une Décoration intelligente," L'Art Sacré,
September–October, 1949, p. 8.

are pained by the contrast, indeed the contradiction, between the picture of Catholicism here presented to us and
that by which we live. But when the building has been
thought out as a whole, with everything in equilibrium,
reflecting a balanced view of dogma and the Christian life,
a sense of peace and joy is ours. It is thus that decoration
can be both intelligent and persuasive[24] without direct
catechetical intent.

Church decoration must edify and instruct, but it must
do so in the same way that the liturgy does—with an intention not so much to educate as to help us contemplate for
ourselves. The Council of Trent insisted that the purpose
of ceremonial is to help us contemplate what the liturgy is
celebrating. If we are to be helped to contemplate, then an
atmosphere is the first thing to be supplied, and this is the
primary purpose of decoration. Père Roguet makes it quite
plain that in order to achieve this he would far rather see
nonrepresentational art in church than the sort of unre-
strained representational art we see in most of our churches
today. The ideal, of course, is to create the right atmosphere
with recognizable representational art, since this evokes
the mysteries of our salvation more explicitly. But this art
form has suffered for more than a century from three unfortunate traits: sentimentality, anecdotal or chronological
concerns, and didacticism.[25] These three great vices constitute the primary difference between modern iconography

[24] Ibid.
[25] Canon Martimort, in L'Art Sacré, September–October, 1949,
pp. 5, 7.

and that of the Middle Ages, which so beautifully stood up
to the demand of preaching the liturgy required of it.

Sentimentality is the curse of all works of art that are
deliberately designed to help us pray, for when we see what
objects people consider most helpful in this matter, we
must wonder if they have any real conception of prayer. I
am speaking of the sort of rubbish which has been aptly
called *kitsch*, which seems to revel in unreal aspirations and
evasions of reality.[26] These things are taken as much for
granted as air pollution in our industrial areas. And since
sentimentality in prayer is so much accepted, it is very difficult to try to do away wth it without scandalizing the
people in whose lives it is so familiar and so cherished;
these objections would do no good, because no one would
understand our criticisms. Perhaps the only thing we can
do is try to correct the popular idea of prayer by encouraging the faithful to find their satisfaction in the liturgy instead of in their own private sentimental devotion.

Anecdotal concerns characterize a faith that is not sufficiently strong to plumb the mysteries it accepts. Such a
faith inevitably stops at the external and accidental. This
has its unfortunate consequences in art. Christianity is essentially historical, of course, but the reality it makes incarnate in time is an eternal mystery; and when the temporal aspect is involved, as it is in art, it must be so presented that it guides the mind to what is contained therein
—the substance of things hoped for. Each episode of the
Gospel is important, but it is important because when faith

[26] F. Demenge, "Le Kitsch dans l'Art et la Vie chrétienne," *L'Art
Sacré*, November–December, 1950.

has penetrated its innermost content we can contemplate fully all that is signified in the mystery. The superficial mind, on the other hand, is interested only in the external trappings of the episode, and never gets to the bottom of what is signified. All it wants is local color. The Church, however, expects the arts to address themselves to our faith —she asks for more than a photograph of Christ's death on Calvary, for instance, to see what Our Lady saw when she was at the foot of the cross. She asks for something more in a series of church windows than "the history of the diocese of Parenzo and of all its saints."[27] She sees no point in having a set of murals around the walls representing the administration of the sacraments,[28] for it is what lies behind the sacraments, their signification, that the painter must evoke.

The concentration on the *teaching function* of art comes from another form of insufficient faith, which tends to lose the essential mystery through a preoccupation with schematic formulas and clear-cut analyses. The type of instruction we associate with the classroom is bound, for the sake of clarity, to put everything in neat systems, but such a schematic treatment is only justified if the living unity of faith is clearly perceived by both the master and those he instructs.[29] A *fortiori*, in the church, where the celebration of the mysteries comes first, its decoration must help those present to

[27] A fictitious example given by Martimort, in *L'Art Sacré*, September–October, 1949, p. 5.
[28] This is the subject of the paintings in the transept of Saint-Ferdinand-des-Ternes in Paris.
[29] Martimort, in *L'Art Sacré*, September–October, 1949.

contemplate the mysteries at the altar and thus come to an experience of the living God. This is the principle which should unify the art of a church. No logical analysis can take the place of this goal. Large doctrinal frescoes of the twelve articles of the creed, the beatitudes, and the virtues are pathetic in every way. There is no point to an endless repetition of the catechism. What the faithful need is to be fed on the Word of God and to share in the mysteries of salvation. The mute preaching of murals and windows is not meant to take us back to the classroom or give us professorial abstractions or pious reveries, but rather to present the major themes of the faith exactly as the believer contemplates them and lives by them in the Christian community. Iconography is like preaching. It is only really good when the preacher drops his theoretical exposé and becomes the herald who proclaims the mystery of salvation[30] according to the needs of the assembly before him.

Pius XII in *Mediator Dei* considered it a duty to "correct the erroneous piety of those who offer a quantity of pictures and statues, even on the altar, to the faithful for devotion." One must have a crucifix for the altar, and there should be a few pictures; it would be very odd for a church to have no picture or statue of Our Lady or of its patron saint. What we must put an end to is the acquisition of many cheap statues instead of one good original. It is customary in our time to put secondary devotions first, giving priority over the mass to practices which are sometimes not even commendable. Such an abuse shows an excessive attachment

[30] See Louis Bouyer, in *La Maison-Dieu*, no. 16, pp. 12, 58.

to secondary means. Protestants accuse us of idolatry, which is probably an exaggeration, but may not be so in every case. Any excessive attachment to devotional pictures and statues demands rectification. Pious materialism gives rise to an increasing flood of objects that are sentimental, sensual, and often vulgar. On this lowest level of all we can no longer speak of "sacred art" since there is no art there at all, and certainly nothing sacred.

St. John of the Cross, following the teaching of the Council of Trent, reminds us that pictures are very useful for bringing God and the saints to mind and for awakening devotion, but this depends on whether we use the pictures properly.[31] He classes them among the things which rouse our devotion through our feelings.[32] That is, their purpose is devotion, and the means to that end is our feelings. The end and the means would seem to involve two contrary dispositions as far as works of art are concerned. On the one hand, we should find them moving, even touching, so that we may be roused to devotion. On the other hand, we should not allow the painting and our appreciation of it to distract us from the living, spiritual element the picture is meant to convey. But there should in fact be no contradiction involved, for it is our task, to raise our minds to what is represented in the picture, directing all our love and fervor to God by devout mental prayer. Far from distracting us, a picture which is deeply moving helps us toward this end, provided it really does indicate the direction we

[31] *The Ascent of Mt. Carmel*, bk. III, pt. 2, chap. 36.
[32] *Ibid.*, chap. 34.

must take toward God. Whether or not it makes this direction clear is a question that needs much discussion, and we
shall in fact come back to this subject in a later chapter.

For a picture to have value for the faithful, it must have
this touching, moving quality. Christians in a working parish
will want a St. Joseph who expresses the dignity of work and
a simple, authentic way of life that is firmly based on a contemplative outlook. The Christian workman has a right to a
representation that expresses all this. Our conversation with
God is an essential feature of the incarnate sphere in which
we live, so that our stations of the cross, our crucifixes and
madonnas must all be able to summon up our love and direct
it to its goal. If the works of art that we find in church really
do draw us into a contemplation of the Christian mystery instead of offering us a few more or less sentimental thoughts, it
is because they engender an atmosphere that corresponds in
a perceptible way to the mystery itself.

Preaching and teaching that inspire real devotion can
only be brought about if there is a definite atmosphere in
the church, and the creation of this atmosphere is the chief
function of sacred art. This atmosphere can be created
without representational art of any sort. The entire framework of the church and everything in it should bear the
impress of something divine—there should be a sacred character about the whole and its component parts. And here
we must observe that the sacred character in question is
not a goal which the artist is to seek consciously and
deliberately. As we have said, the first aim is to establish an
atmosphere of prayer, but this atmosphere cannot be deliberately sought after. It must come as a gratuitous gift, an

overflow, a definite grace. Human industry, unaided by God, cannot produce a sacred work.

It is a common misapprehension that the sacred character of a work of art is something objective, that is, immediately obvious to everyone. To analyze this commonly accepted opinion, we would do well to begin with a consideration that is the fruit of many people's experience, that every work of art worthy of the name bears some impress of what we can call a sacred character. Paul Jamot once pointed out that all sorts of things that once seemed thoroughly profane—dance tunes, modes of dress—are anything but profane when the period to which they belonged has passed away; they are art. All of us can make this observation in any museum. I do not mean that we should visit museums in a nostalgic mood, to hanker after the things of the past; we should rather simply examine the products of past generations as objects, just as they are. As works of art, they give us an impression of having been gathered up out of the flux of time and placed on some transcendent level, for these are things that once belonged to the superficial aspects of a certain phase of history and society. All we have to do is lift them bodily from that phase. Their sacred character becomes all the more marked, of course, as soon as we put them to some religious use. A profane musical air can be turned into the theme of a mass or into a hymn like the *Conditor alme siderum*;[33] and how often have we been impressed by the dignity of some splendid armchair in the

[33] Joseph Samson, *Musique et Vie intérieure* (Paris: La Colombe, 1951), gives further instances on pp. 138, 140, 180, 184.

sanctuary, only to remember as an afterthought that it was designed to grace one of the exquisite salons of the eighteenth century?

Joseph Samson has listed various qualities perceptible in every real work of art which are capable of awakening in us a contact with the sacred. He suggests silence, recollection, and lyricism. "Painting an apple or a dish or a pipe," he says, "composing a piece of music about coffee or tobacco, as did J. S. Bach, can only result in a work of art to the degree in which some lyrical vibration is transmitted to us by means of harmony, line, and color. When the artist laughs, he laughs like the gods." This assertion has in it a deep intuition of what lyricism really means. "Underlying every activity of thought and feeling, there is a lyrical expression in the heart of man which is the Creator singing through him. As God sings, he enraptures the heart of man to sing with him, making the creature rejoice and dance and open his soul to the whole world."[34] It is at this level that art is created. Its value as art derives from this Source which flows through it. And this is the meaning of sacred.

From here we can speculate along several lines of thought with regard to the "otherness" involved in artistic creation. First, every artistic activity means a transcendence of the data of nature, and when it achieves this successfully it is bound to communicate to the beholder or the listener some idea of transcendence. Again, we may say that nature, which is God's artistry, bears the impress of his perfection, but this impress is hidden from men's eyes by the blinding dis-

[34] *Ibid.*, pp. 174–177.

tractions of everyday life. The artist who takes up Cézanne's cry, "See the work of God," awakens perception from its apathy. Finally, God is the source of all beauty and of every noble and pure expression of this beauty. To express beauty is to underline a divine attribute and thus to do a sacred work. This is the meaning of Michelangelo's "Every good painting is, in itself, something both noble and devotional."[35]

In spite of this, it is a commonly accepted opinion that the sacred character of a work of art can be immediately identified with certain styles. In architecture, for instance, the touchstone is an ogival arch, so miscalled. In the representational arts, it is some particular technique like that of Byzantine painters or the severe lines of the Beuronese. Some people would even go so far as to say that a work violating these accepted canons cannot possibly be sacred in character. This is the artistic pharisaism which results from a refusal to accept certain styles because they are associated with the profane. In this way, purely arbitrary restrictions on art can be canonized in the course of time.

But we have only to open our eyes to negate any such theory. When we really look, we find the sacred in such an infinite variety of forms and in so many different historical and ethnic styles that we cannot bear being tied down to our own limited culture and its canons, or rather to its habits and prejudices. A genuine feeling for the sacred and the transcendent should be enough to put us on our guard

[35] These words of Michelangelo's were taken down by Francisco de Hollanda, a Portuguese, during an interview he had with the artist. See *Quatre Dialogues sur la Peinture de Francisco de Hollanda*, tr. into French by Léo Rouanet (1911), pp. 29–30.

against any rigorous systemization of forms. It is transcendence itself, even more than the great variety of forms that transcendence assumes, which makes it impossible to lay down any exclusive stylistic forms. The sacred is immutable and beyond all styles.

Provided we avoid any rigid and exclusive system of forms, in theory there is no reason why we should not keep our preferences for certain figures, certain rhythms, certain techniques, in the hope that these will constitute some sort of language for expressing the sacred. But this is almost impossible in practice, since the means we use to convey our expression of the sacred will inevitably become stereotyped and lose their vigor, and with it their aptitude to be given life by our feelings.

In our time, every artificial system of artistic forms becomes a sort of Volapük or Esperanto—either that or, as when it copies the past, a mere reconstruction of a dead language. The hieratic arts of the past, far from persuading us to copy them line by line, tell us all the time that plastic language is only of value when it is living, fertile, and so natural that the artist feels and conceives his creation according to this language. Byzantine art at its best, for instance, may seem to some of us arbitrarily conceived, but in fact it is an exact counterpart of the creative spirit of its time. There were certain periods and places in the past when quality did not suffer from the presence of strong and deeply formed habits, so long as these were living habits. In the manners of that day, custom interested the moralist to the exclusion of innovation, and the same was true of the artist. One has the impression that his whole preoccupation was to conform to the canons of the beautiful and to the accepted procedure in manner and style.

But we must not suppose that the artist had only to obey these laws to produce a beautiful and sacred work. In those days, as in ours, the rules of art could only aid a genius when they were in accord with the deepest inclinations of mankind, when man himself gave life to these laws by his own responsiveness. In ancient Egypt, or China, or the Eastern Roman Empire, or during the Middle Ages in the West, there was far more harmony than conflict between the rules of art and the creative demands of the artist, contrary to the situation today. The reason for this harmony was that both the rules of art and the creative artist visibly reflected the harmony of the universe. But in our time all has changed, including the social conditions of the artist's life and the psychic conditions of sensitivity and artistic creation. The canons, the conventions of style, the clear-cut and yet complex symbolism, the actual processes involved in making a work of art, all of which were once considered necessary for a sacred work, today mostly seem artificial. Even in the past, these factors led to decadence and sterility when they had outworn their usefulness. Since nowadays these things are not part of a living tradition, they can only be of the nature of archeological reconstruction.

Now, since it is obvious that the hallowed forms of the past no longer have the power to confer a sacred character on a work of art, can we nevertheless maintain that there are certain features which do at least summon up the idea of something religious? For instance, we are not being purely arbitrary when we drape a catafalque in black; there is something objectively funereal about black. One could possibly drape a catafalque in gold, but certainly not in some gay contemporary pattern. Here there is at least some objective correspondence between a convention and a fact of the spiritual order.

We can possibly go so far as to discern three planes in a discussion of what constitutes the sacred in art. There is the level of what is immediately grasped as deeply sacred. There is the superficially sacred or what is accepted as sacred through habit. Then there is an intermediate level, distinct from the deep as from the superficial, which is constituted by a kind of correspondence between the physical and the spiritual realities. Here we are conscious of the evocative power of certain physical qualities. In works of art these qualities are the effects of a particular "mode of being" of the artist, which consists of a kind of orientation of the artist's creative gifts toward the transcendent.

Generally speaking, art contacts the sacred whenever it achieves completion, whenever it achieves detachment, and whenever it breaks with the banal outlook on life. This is the deep level. The paths along which it is directed may differ. Our judgment may be the product of convention, of the episodic nature of our civilization by comparison with eternity; nevertheless, this is the milieu in which we work out our destiny, and in which we desire genuinely sacred works. The arts are really only sacred insofar as they arouse in us the sense of the numinous which they find in these bounds.

We can normally discern a difference of meaning among the words *sacred*, *religious*, *moral*, and *Christian*, but it is the artist's task to make all four coincide. The sacred, simply as transcendence, may exist before religion, and it can be immoral, purely instinctive, and even perverse. We Catholics are not always reminded of God's transcendence by our church worship, or church decoration, or even by the worshipers and ministers we find in those churches. Only Christ can make the sacred coincide exactly with the moral, for he by his Incarnation has made the transcendent into something interior to ourselves. Every personal moral act, a fortiori every act of worship, should attest its transcendent quality. In Christianity the highest virtue is love, which is both divine and brotherly. Thus the sacred does not lose its segregating quality but gains tremendously because, according to Christ, the principle of all segregation is divine love. Love is as strong and as terrible as death. Yet it unites even more than it separates. "Since the Incarnation," says Père Doncœur, "the sacred has involved communion much more than prohibition. Christ does not consecrate bread that will be shut up in the ark as 'loaves of proposition.' The bread he gives us is to be distributed and eaten. The sacred is no longer an inert and remote object but a life-giving and interior principle. Love is now the center around which the world revolves, and only love can define what is segregated. Everything love commands is holy. Everything that wounds love is sacrilege. Everything is pure through charity."[36]

The sacred is determined by what God really is. He is the Deus immensae majestatis of the Te Deum—the thrice holy one of Isaias. He is not a blind force which is vaguely

[36] Père Paul Doncœur, Péguy, la Révolution et le Sacré (1941), pp. 108, 114.

at large in creation. He is infinitely "other" to his creatures and incapable of being mixed with them. Yet he is incarnate as Christ and he is the Spirit given to men.

Thus faith gives a definite form to our idea of what is sacred, and this form is not an artificial one, since faith is truly our second nature. Faith teaches us the truth about God, and the first thing it teaches about him is our fundamental attitude toward him—a realization of total nothingness. In the Middle Ages it was called *resilitio in propriam parvitatem*—a withdrawal into one's own littleness—implying reverence, holy fear, and adoration. Here is the terrifying experience of the God of infinite greatness. For the sinner it means the fear of punishment which is separation from God—*timor separationis*—and the fear of sinning further—*timor offensae*. For the soul who can perceive the gravity of knowing God even faintly, it is *timor adequationis*. The traditional analysis of holy fear is very near Otto's conception of the *mysterium tremendum*. God is both *mirum*, the absolutely Other, inspiring us with wonder and awe and *fascinosum*, exercising a magnetic attraction, a desire for union.[37]

There is no real opposition between holy fear and love, since this fear contains the desire for communion with God. Love, on the other hand, is never without holy fear, the only fear incompatible with love being servile fear. The more we love, the more we realize how infinite is the distance between us and God. The great revelation of Chris-

[37] Père Mennessier points this out in *La Religion*, I, 308–309 (tr. into French of the *Summa Theologiae* by the Revue des Jeunes).

tianity, the certitude that God, despite all appearances to
the contrary, is love, is bound to introduce an element of
tenderness into what is sacred. But this must never be allowed to diminish our reverence for the sacred, whether it
be in religion or in art, for if it does, it is bound to render
them equally mediocre. The sacred character of a work of
art depends ultimately on the presence of these dispositions
of holy fear and love in the artist. The technique he uses
must be strong and pure, but above all these dispositions
must guide him in the very act of creation. Is "beauty" a
way toward the sacred, or is it a hindrance to it?

To clarify this issue, we must first agree on what is "beautiful" in a given work of art. Far too many people are willing
to say that they find beauty wherever they can find the accepted conventions. But true beauty in art, just like the
sacred character itself, is something gratuitous that over-
flows from the artist's own mode of being, and passes into
act in the moment of generation. This mode of being is a
demand for the absolute which the work of art will reveal
in its own way. The artist's soul needs to reach out to the
very limits of itself. Therefore, the artist is unfaithful to his
essential self if he falls back on conventions. In a work of
art there is an absolute, there is freedom, and there is a
sharp perception of the human spirit, awakening and wak-
ing others. Our eyes are still closed if we let "beauty" be
nothing for us but convention, art nothing but artifice.
There is something of convention in every observer's appreciation, but only because there is an element of habit in
every human act. A man, to be a man, must live as a free
agent, not as an automaton; a creator, to be a creator, must

re-examine everything that presents itself to him, infuse his own life into it, and subject it to the service of a new vision, one new with the ever-recurring newness of his own life.

To be stamped with a *sacred* character a work of art must before all else have some *character*. In earlier periods habit and sensitivities were more in accord than they are today. Most modern artists are lacking in that sensitivity to forms which once inspired every artisan, however untalented; on the other hand, a very few great artists have had that sensitivity hypertrophied and overstimulated by the overwhelming exploits of contemporary art. And this is the condition which, whether we like it or not, influences sacred art in our time. It is this condition that demands us to seek out the very principles of sacred art. In less abnormal times, the answer was obvious, and the question remained unformulated. The principle is always to be found in the creative force of an art shaped from within by the sense of the sacred. Traditional techniques are only useful if they can be revivified through this creative force. The results may be a poverty of beauty, and of every other lovely quality we associate with golden ages of art; or it can happen that art may still claim to possess the riches of bygone days. The more an artist refuses to accept this fact, the more he must betray the sacred character that was once there, because it was born of spontaneity. But on the other hand, every perceptible quality that is expressed with sincerity and transfigured by the spirit will always be able to evoke the transcendental.

2

The Art of the Incarnate Word

"There is no art that is specifically Christian, just as there is
no style that is specifically Christian. . . . It is impossible to
paint a 'Christian' landscape, but it is possible to look at a
landscape in a Christian way. Although Bossuet may have
looked at mountains in a very different way from St. Matthew, the mountain, for both of them, is first and foremost the place from whence salvation comes. In other
words there is a specifically Christian reaction to nature,
and a Christian answer to nature in our hearts." So writes
Joseph Samson.[1] One of the two recorded sayings of Fra
Angelico sums up the whole question: "If you would paint
the things of Christ, you must live with Christ." If we can
realize fully what is demanded of the artist in virtue of the
image of Christ that he bears in his soul, we can put out of
our minds completely any idea that such and such an art
form is the right one for a Christian artist to use.

The Word of God took flesh at Nazareth, and from that
moment every gesture in every trivial household task be-

[1] Joseph Samson, *Musique et Vie intérieure* (Paris: La Colombe,
1951), pp. 224, 226, 228, 246.

came divinized. Until the end of time, the Word will penetrate and permeate every small detail of our human existence. There is nothing in life that the Holy Spirit cannot transfigure for us—nothing that we can put aside as impossible for us to transform.

If the artist's eye is sound, then the whole body of his art will live in the light.[2] "Love and do what you will. . . ." St. Augustine's words have a similar application, for if we really love God, then we shall will what he wills. If not, we can achieve nothing. There is something in the Christian outlook which is genuinely childlike, a sense of seriousness. A true Christian, like a child, can deflate false prestige, and put his finger on the exact place where all beings are caught up in the life of God. His instinct is unerring. God's work can be recognized in what is humblest in every created thing. The characteristic of Christian art is a clear perception, a sure grasp which finds in all things what God loves most in them. It holds on to this quality, and with it makes all things new.

This trait of childlike earnestness is poles apart from the pseudo-seriousness of adults. Christian seriousness means that the soul is not distracted by an irrelevance, but esteems everything at its true worth. This attitude has given us Chartres, the sculpture of Pisano, and the medieval parish churches. Vision, perception, aesthetic goals, all these may be widely different; yet in every case one will find that the creators of these various works have only expressed what they themselves have felt. This is what everyone loves about

[2] Matt. 6:22.

the "Nativity" of Georges de la Tour—even though it is not a Nativity in the real sense, but only a picture of two peasant women and a sleeping child. The reason it is so much more than merely another genre painting is because the painter has seen and makes us see the eternal reality which is present in any scene of a child asleep on its mother's lap, and which, ever since Bethlehem, contains a mystery, a sacred mystery.

Christian seriousness is, if you will, the ability to find what is eternally valid in every instant since the moment God the Eternal came into time. Such a revelation of infinite depth is all the more striking when we compare it with its artistic opposite—the exaltation of the fugitive and momentary, the external and the circumstantial. To the degree that an artist is faithful to this revelation will his work be sacred and Christian. Like a child, seriously intent on work or play, his task is to discover the manner in which God's creative love is expressed in the world; when he has discovered it, he will deliver himself of his work as spontaneously as if it were a song.

Although Christianity prescribes no forms of art as specifically its own, it suggests an ideal and defines certain limits. Its ideal is what one might call supernaturalism, or perhaps more precisely mystical naturalism. Christian art must be the most realistic and at the same time the most spiritual possible. It is not a compromise between these two but an intense fusion of both. The Word was made flesh,[3] but this was no mere juxtaposition of flesh and

[3] John 1:14.

Word. Christ, the only being who is both God and man, is the unique mediator[4] between God and us, and there is no other. He came to us and took our human flesh to himself, so that our flesh is transformed by the Word, and our vocation is that we be made divine.[5] The more fully art can express this transfiguration of mankind and creation, the more it can fulfill its function. Art is meant to reveal the spiritual, the divine, by using the appearances of "carnal" nature and things of the perceptible order.

It goes without saying that such an ideal can be fully realized only by the divine art of God. We have to be content with what mere human art can do. Our art will be essentially a modest and unpretentious thing, its only possible greatness being the quality of its works. Christian art means the most perfect possible resemblance to the Incarnation of the Word, namely, the spiritualized flesh. An art that deliberately "spiritualizes" its subject matter is usually a mistake. To despise the flesh usually implies a misapprehension of the real nature of spirit. The real Christian artist could never yearn for some immaterial beauty, though when we look at some of the popular, insipid religious art of the last two centuries we can see that the motive behind it is not so much a faith in the living God as a vague deism. Christian art could not possibly confuse the supernatural with the abstract (I do not mean the art called abstract), because the supernatural has come down to us as someone supremely tangible. We have seen him with our eyes, we have looked upon him, and our hands have touched the

[4] I Tim. 2:5.
[5] See my article in Vie Spirituelle, November, 1949.

Word of Life.[6] Christianity, which is the true and perfect monotheism, thus requires that art develop to its full flowering, while Judaism and Islam confine it within narrow limits. The reason is simple: Christianity is the religion of the Word made flesh.

This Christian artistic development has been faithful to its own inner logic. The mysteries of our salvation happened as history, in well-defined episodes that speak to us through our senses. Therefore, the representation they require in art must be of the most perceptible kind possible, while at the same time it must direct our attention to the purely spiritual mystery it embodies. The Christian ideal in art is to exalt the possibilities that each work of art has of also being the incarnation of a word—the human word, which possesses its own spark of infinity.

The Incarnation makes us consider first and foremost the prime importance of facts. Gnosticism was always suspect in the Church, even though there is a genuinely Christian gnosis which can act as a leaven in the uninspired mass of the Church. The more spiritually-minded need something mystical which counteracts a too down-to-earth and unimaginative acceptance of the realities of faith. Loosely speaking, there is a kind of gnosis, esoteric no doubt but essential to the church, which deepens[7] our appreciation of the mysteries of faith. This is the celebrated *mystica theologia*, the holy wisdom which the Church has always rightly prized. The spiritual sense of Scripture, to be the true one, must be drawn from the strictly literal sense of Scripture,

[6] I John 1:1.
[7] Col. 3:10.

and nothing more. In just the same way, the gnosis we have
in mind is neither added to nor substituted for the common
teaching of the Church. It does not claim to come from
any other source than approved doctrine or to be in any way
superior to it. It "confesses that Jesus Christ has come in
the flesh,"[8] nothing more. It was born from the pierced
side of the new Adam with the water of baptism and the
blood of the eucharist. It is directed to the practical works
of love, and never theorizes for the sake of theorizing. It
has to put charity first because, in the end, we shall not be
judged on our beauty but only on our charity, not on our
lofty conceptions but on whether we have done the truth.[9]

Our contemporaries often prefer gnosis to charity, considering the truths of faith, as they are commonly understood, to be altogether too materialistic. Those who give
these truths only a symbolic value imagine they are putting
them to a better use than are the general run of men. René
Guénon was writing in this vein when he said, "Christianity, at least in its external and popular aspect, seems to have
forgotten the symbolic value of the cross. For most people
it is only the sign of an act accomplished in time." How true
indeed! What else would a Christian wish to know but
Jesus, and Jesus crucified,[10] in order to share in his sufferings and to benefit by the power of his resurrection? The
only reason we can speak of Christian symbolism is because
of this one essential truth. Any symbolism that refers us

[8] I John 4:2.
[9] John 3:21.
[10] I Cor. 2:2, Phil. 3:10.

to Jesus and his cross must make a deep appeal to every Christian, but God forbid that Jesus Christ himself should be regarded as a symbol by means of which we rise to something higher! This, one imagines, is what Pius XII had in mind when he condemned what he called "excessive symbolism."[11] Since he was writing with the mass of the faithful in mind, he presumably meant a symbolism that required some initiation into its meaning other than that which every Christian might learn from the catechism.

The religion of the Incarnate Word requires that iconography be fundamentally an elucidation of a narrative. From the earliest days of Christian art, in the catacombs, for instance, we find simple symbols like the fish accompanying such Biblical scenes as the Last Supper. As soon as the faith emerged from the catacombs the walls of the basilicas were covered with great cycles of sacred history.[12] We find the culmination of this movement in the Scrovegni Chapel at Padua where, because of the small proportions of the building and the simplicity of the methods used, we are startled by the intense realism of the work. The faithful are gathered in the procession which is formed by the figures on either side, while God the Father hovers overhead, with the Annunciation taking place beneath him. At the altar, Christ's sacrifice is depicted beneath its Old Testament type. As we leave the chapel, we are reminded at the west door of the culmination of history in the Last Judgment.

[11] From the encyclical *Mediator Dei*.
[12] The Synod of Constantinople in 692 gave its approbation to historical subjects in preference to emblems (Bayart, ed., *Dictionnaire de Droit Canonique*, II, col. 272).

Today we are more conscious of the danger attendant upon this iconography—of reducing historical events to mere anecdotes. This anecdotal treatment like the ultra-naturalism and sentimentality that correspond to it, has debased much religious art. Even at the end of the Middle Ages, popular taste favored the familiar, the tender, and the touching, and although there is a danger here as noted above, we must not forget that such qualities may intensify our awareness that the redemption is basically historical and factual.

Pius XII did not, we must remember, condemn only the excesses of symbolism; he also condemned the excesses of realism. This is not surprising, since there is nothing Christian about depicting visible realities without any suggestion of what lies beyond them. Mere realism, such as we find in the work of Bonnat, Cormon, and Jean-Paul Laurens, is a negation of art. Nor can the sentimentality of the theme or of the "expression" give any truly spiritual value to painting or sculpture which is too realistic. But it is precisely the sort of picture which is absolutely photographic, and at the same time unrealistic in its pious whimsicality, that most people expect to see in church. That there is great realism in church art, no one will deny. We have our Caravaggio—to say nothing of the Caravaggeschi—but there is a world of difference between the heights of Caravaggio and the depths of the Carracci.

We are meant to "restore all things in Christ,"[13] because the Incarnation involved everything human. Everything, as

[13] Eph. 1:10.

Saint Paul says, is Christian—except sin.[14] So broad a conception demands infinite diversity for its expression. Any one style is inadequate to express the transcendent Christian revelation; and this is only one of many factors that necessitates a variety of styles. Another factor is that there is an infinity of human contexts in which art and its subject matter must take shape. Faith cannot be tied to any one social regime or political party or economic program. It must be free, precisely in order that it may instill life into other regimes and programs. Faith can never favor exclusively any one system of philosophy or theology or liturgy. Still less could it ever canonize one single art form. There are too many unrealized potentialities to be drawn out of Christianity for any one of them to be exclusively favored and encouraged. There are so many mansions in the house of Christian art that we must never presume to shut up any one of them or close our eyes to the possibility of many more being opened to us in the future.

A Christian must love diversity. Totalitarian unity, so prevalent in our time in politics and in art, is inconceivable to the Christian mentality. "It takes all sorts to make a world," and charity should make us happy to find that others are different from ourselves and from each other.

[14] Eph. 3:18, where St. Paul obviously means that the love of Christ has no limits. But while one accepts the literal sense of this verse, one can still benefit by the traditional exegesis (see St. Thomas's commentaries on St. Paul's Epistles), according to which the "height" involved is Christ's divinity, the "depth" his mercy, the "breadth" his humanity, which is that of universal mankind, and the "length" the dimension of time, in which Christ is unendingly the same.

The insufficiency of each of us as individuals points to our need for one another.

Art cannot be fully Christian, even when it has embraced all this diversity, until it has learned to tell the world that Christ is glorified. Art has, as it were, to reflect onto this world some of the splendor that shines from Christ's face.[15] And here there is danger of a new pharisaism, for when art succeeds in doing this, the splendor it achieves seems to be the goal of its whole aspiration, and the means that enables art to aim so high tend to become taken for granted, as if they were purely human possessions independent of God the giver. Even if the artist can accept his achievement as the result of a grace, he may still think of it as a due reward for his labors. The Ravenna mosaics, the façade of Rheims, the dome of St. Peter's show us what art can do in the way of reflecting Christ's glory down into our world. A truly Christian artist must be enlightened by the aureole of Christ's glory.

The worst corruption of all is the corruption of the best. The most horrible imposture of all is that art which paints and sculpts a glory that is not the outcome of the artist's talents aided by grace but of the artist's efforts alone. We have seen in the Basilica of Lisieux the results of artists' pretensions to create a new St. Peter's thus unaided.

The sort of art that depicts Christ's glory is certainly possible; indeed, it is one of the necessary summits of the art of the Incarnation. The successes of this art are very rare, however, and very dangerous. But if the artist has a true concep-

[15] II Cor. 4:6.

tion of God's transcendence, he will express grandeur in so humble a way that he will put all academic imitations of grandeur to shame. Indeed, this academic grandeur would be quite unbearable to artists who had realized the essence of the Cross, the *kenosis* of Christ,[16] without which no art can be truly Christian. This is the indispensable realization, although it must never overwhelm the artist's whole imagination, as it did Rembrandt's, so that his works do not reflect that true glory of which we have been speaking. Christian art must maintain a balance, and see to it that no one trait dominates the others.

A pseudo-Christian humanism conceives God's perfections as the perfections of creatures magnified. This is the great temptation for the academic painter. In fact, God's creatures hardly resemble God at all, even though they are made in his image and likeness,[17] for there is only an analogical similarity between the Creator and his work, while their dissimilarities are almost everything. The religion of the humanist is likely to be merely an inflation of the human mode of grasping reality: Christ is simply another Apollo or Jupiter; the sublime is mere bombast and pretension. Genius may save the painter—here we may think of Rubens—but the underlying humanism is as much a denial of true art as it is of true Christianity.

Everything is Christian except sin. Sin is always an exile to a land which is distant from God. And the exile is from the kingdom of God, the inner kingdom of the soul. Self-sufficiency is the great sin against Christian art, and the

16 The *kenosis* of which St. Paul speaks in Phil. 2:7.
17 Gen. 1:26.

more ambitious the artist's project, the greater risks he runs. The more the artist is concerned for his own achievement, the more does he ignore the one thing necessary. Instead of the triumph of Christ over the contingent universe, he will show us a new primitivism without any appeal to the senses; instead of Christ's beauty, a benighted pedantry propped up by academic theories.[18]

At different times in the history of art, one discovers a varying stress on one of the two principal emphases that the Incarnation makes inevitable. On the one hand, the upheaval caused in history by the intervention of God can disrupt art; on the other, the fact that God has "naturalized" himself in our human world may draw art into a kind of euphoria. In this second emphasis, Christian civilization and culture are at their height, and God's relationship with mankind is visualized as a conversation. It is not surprising to find in the Florentine Quattrocento that a favorite theme is that of "holy conversations" between saints and the holy family. It follows logically from the fact that the institutions established by the supernatural in society are like the beneficial shade of the young trees of Paradise. In different periods of history we can find these compositions, harmoniously united in their form and coloring and exuding an air of peace and relaxation. We find it in Enguerrand Carton, Memling, Fra Angelico, and Raphael. This is the gentle, soft climate of art that many people believe to be the only possible one for Christian art.

[18] See my article "Explication de la Décadence: L'Académisme et ses Méfaits," L'Art Sacré, October, 1947.

But at the present time we are more conscious of the other emphasis—the formidable advent of God among us. This gives a violent shock to our art, so great that we feel instinctively that it should reveal the faith we ought to have, a faith strong enough "to bring about the end of the world."[19] The shock is all the greater since ours is a period of intense striving toward the absolute. It tends to discourage any evocation of mystery by direct means, and encourages a backward art, in which the soul intensely concerned with the absolute evokes a sense of God in what is most wretched in the world.

This extreme could not bear weight, but it is at least in accord with the logic of the Incarnation. On any question of our relationship with God, the voice of prophecy is more authoritative than that of the bureaucrat. But the prophet must be genuine, and this is not always the case. If a prophetic movement is true in its sources, it must seek to remain so throughout—throughout the artist's work, which will reflect the authentic aspirations of his fellow men. The more he seeks to find what these authentic aspirations are, however, the greater is his risk of being an imposter. Our desire for the absolute will be short-lived if it fails to recognize that it must survive in the midst of all those other claims upon us, which are so very different from our longing for the absolute. All we can do is maintain our balance amid the many realities which we cannot reconcile and which we must always accept in their ensemble. For the Incarnation implies that God's transcendence is always disturbing our established conceptions and at the same time, since this

19 L. Venturi, *Rouault* (Paris: Skira, 1949).

transcendence is immanent, binding us more closely to
reality and to one another. Christianity means a deep familiarity with everything holy, a familiarity which many regard
as a profanation. (We need only think of popular devotions,
of the normal Christian accommodation to the standards of
this world, and of the temptations of a secularized Christian
humanism.)

But at the same time, Christ is the infinite Word before
whom all the powers of creation tremble; he is the creative
Word, the Word dividing the soul from the mind.[20] And as
man, he is the greatest worshiper of God. Our Christian art
must therefore never lose its function of emphasizing the
remoteness of God from man. We must accept the irrecon-
cilable demands of a Christian art, those which come from
the height and proclaim Christ's glory and those which
come from the depth, from the depth of all wretchedness
and from the *kenosis* of Christ. On the face of it, no distortion or pathos designed to express this height and depth
could really be thought of as exaggerated. It could only be
excessive in relation to the plastic values of the work of art,
which must always be faithful to Christ in the divine dignity which he never lost and in the abjection which he willingly embraced. Depth and height are in fact the same
dimension seen in two different lights. Christ goes down to
the deepest depths of misery, taking with him all the
treasures of knowledge and wisdom. He goes up to the
heights at his Ascension and glorifies every conceivable human misery, except sin. Do these contrary and simultaneous
demands of a Christian art cancel each other out? Is the

[20] Heb. 4:12.

Christian artist engaged in an undertaking which is fundamentally impossible?

Most people prefer compromise and eclecticism. They like to think that one might combine Raphael's drawing with Titian's color and Correggio's grace with Michelangelo's power. They imagine that if they were to combine the façade of Rheims with the nave of Amiens, they would get something more splendid than either Rheims or Amiens. They fail to realize that each of the two cathedrals represents something which must remain unique in its individuality. The eclectic ideal is quantitative and materialistic; it treats qualities as if they were quantities to be added together in order to produce a larger sum. The eclectic is always, ultimately, a man of half-measure and compromise, and his work is bound to fail because it makes bedfellows of incompatibilities. If the eclectic could really see the realities involved, any illusion of being able to produce an eclectic work would disappear. A true understanding of Christianity should be enough to make the eclecticism to which it seems to be fatally condemned impossible, for in Christ every vocation is something completely individual.

When the Church goes about canonizing a saint, she asks if the saint has shown signs of all the virtues, for she cannot conceive of offering a mutilated spirituality as an example. But in every saint, the individual's temperament and vocation will ensure that some virtue will dominate. In the arts, it is even more difficult to develop every different quality, since the work is circumscribed by limits even more constricting than those which define the art of living. The Christian should love diversity, and should resent any vague mixture or compromise in which precious individual differences may be lost. Differences are valuable, and Christianity deems it important that all the various mansions of Christian art should be open to each other as well as to the light they all share. At the same time, it is obvious that each must keep its own special identity, its own incommunicable secret. If it is difficult to descry the plan of all these mansions, it should not be hard to accept the fact that the Architect responsible for them is wise enough to be completely trustworthy. It is a good thing for personalities to be so strongly individual that they will only find peace of soul within the Trinity.

The limits that Christian art must accept are today more pronounced because of their contrast with such alien tendencies as vague spiritualism, recondite or heterodox symbolism, dull naturalism, and pallid academicism (whether pathetically poor or enormously pretentious, whether pseudo-classic, pseudo-primitive, or just "modern"). Within its limits, Christian art can be completely itself, and quite content to be no more. Its inspiration and life principle are in the heights of God and the depths of humanity. Within these limits its field is limitless. It is meant to transcend all bounds except these two, and even when focused on one of these extremes it must always be open to the influences of the other. Grünewald's "Crucifixion" at Colmar radiates splendor even from the depths of its pathos and horror, while in the gentle Fra Angelico one is always aware of the artist's secret perception of the cross. Rouault, at his most violent, is imbued with a wonderful peace, of which we become more and more conscious in his later work.

The best way to understand Christian art is to be able to feel the full force of the liberty of the children of God. But how often liberty is misunderstood! How many men go through life without realizing that it consists in our attachment to the infinite. And in our human history this infinite is crystallized in the person of Christ. When we speak of an attachment to the infinite, we are talking about much more than a theory—it is something factual, possible, real. It is a binding heart to heart; nothing has such a powerful attraction for the heart of man. Being an infinite attraction in effect, it can draw us through everything. Yet it does not set the individual against society. On the contrary, it is the only solution of the conflict, since at the point where our hearts are bound to the heart of Christ the individual is transmuted into a real person who is vitally necessary to society. When God's children have attained their true freedom, they are always enemies of the the sort of institutions that falsely claim to represent the true order. When they recognize the real true order, they are its most devoted servants.

There is an essential gratuity in art which demands that art be one of of man's freest activities. The truth frees us; art need not be chained up in order to be Christian. For those who are fearful, let us point out three requirements by which art resolves its internal struggles and strikes a balance among the imbalances that distort it. There is the fundamental seriousness, the faithfulness to truth's secret demands mentioned at the beginning of this chapter, which must always be borne in mind. This is the most important requirement. The second requirement is the artist's application to his work, and his respect for the materials, the

milieu, and the particular Christian community for whom
his work is destined. Third, there is the Church's own requirement, which we shall consider in the three following
chapters. We must never forget that Christ has exalted the
human person and saved it from anarchy through the
medium of his Church.

It may be useful at this juncture to consider exactly what
we mean by the Christian quality which must fill the artist,
determine his life, and eventually find its way into his work.
We could do this in several ways, but the one I should like
to pursue relies on an examination of the "psychology" of
the gifts of the Holy Spirit. This would seem to be the best
way, since the "spirit of Jesus"[21] is obviously our best guide
for sketching the portrait of a real Christian. We can add to
this the portrait that is offered for us by the beatitudes of
the Gospel, since these constitute the program that Our
Lord himself assigns to every Christian. Finally there is
Mary, whose mission is to form Christ in the faithful. She is
bound to have something illuminating to tell us about the
influence she has on the arts when they are placed under her
tutelage.

We have already spoken of the Holy Spirit's gift of fear,
which is the gift of the sacred par excellence. Christian tradition has significantly distinguished two gifts in it, adding
what is called piety.[22] In piety, the Church sees especially
the implication of our divine adoption: "Now . . . you have
received a spirit of adoption as sons, by virtue of which we

[21] Acts 16:7.
[22] Following the translation of Isaias 11:2 in the Septuagint.

cry, 'Abba, Father!' The Spirit himself gives testimony to our spirit that we are sons of God."[23] Ours must be a filial fear; therefore, it must be a fusion of holy fear and tender piety. We are nothing before God, and at the same time we are his sons.[24] Our conviction of this must be living, spontaneous, and sincere. We need this double gift, which inspires us with a sense of our nothingness and at the same time with a sense of familiar trust.

The first two beatitudes correspond to these gifts.[25] Blessed are those who are poor in Spirit. Blessed are the meek. Spiritual poverty is an introduction to life; it is also an introduction to art. It is implicit in everything we have said so far, but it must be repeated now. If Christians and their pastors had the hearts of really poor people—Christ's poor—the problem of art would be solved.

Meekness is one of the specifically Christian qualities. Christ speaks of his own heart as "meek and humble," and what we should find even more striking is that he says, "Learn from me, for I am meek and humble of heart."[26] Meekness is his justification for being our teacher. Quoting one of the psalms, he adds that meekness is rewarded by "possessing the land." He shows us therefore that art will only convince men, will only touch what belongs to Christ in men's souls, if it is imbued with the meekness of Christ. True meekness is a rare and great quality, and because the corruption of the best is the worst corruption of all, false,

23 Rom. 8:15–16.
24 I John 3:1.
25 Matt. 5:3–4.
26 Matt. 11:29.

saccharin meekness is the most repulsive of all. False meekness has discredited genuine meekness in the eyes of most
men. This is tragic, for true meekness is a gift of the Spirit
which cannot be assumed at will. The Christian artist must
desire it, wait for it, and strive to be worthy of it through
his contemplation of the goodness and kindness of God as
manifest in the Savior.[27]

Thus, the two gifts of spiritual poverty and meekness give
us the right dispositions towards God. There are three more
which help the soul to act like a Christian in this world: the
knowledge which the saints possess of things doomed to die,
fortitude, and counsel. With these go the three beatitudes
which illumine the tragic side of life—blessed are those who
mourn; blessed are those who hunger and thirst after justice;
blessed are the merciful.

The thirst for justice has an immediate application in the
sphere of art, being translated of necessity into a passion for
truth and honesty. For just as in life, in art fortitude and
justice play a central part in maintaining the proper balance.

In Christ, mercy is not one quality among many. It is his
very definition, and explains his being and his destiny. He
is infinite mercy who has come to the rescue of humanity in
its misery, and he continues this redemptive work throughout time by means of his members in the Church. Whereas
indulgence simply minimizes evil and come to terms with
it, mercy sees it in all its horror because Christian revelation
throws more light on it than can the unaided reason. One
may even say that mercy becomes identified with the zeal

27 Tit. 3:4.

for justice, although the meekness of Christ introduces the additional quality of compassion. Love is not sufficiently loved in this world, and when a Christian realizes this fact, his heart must bear the wound of the Spirit forever after. Christian tradition has always recognized that the counsel of the Spirit leads the Christian soul to pity, and that only the Spirit's counsel can teach us to show mercy. It is surely true to say that in works of art which move us deeply we perceive the effects of this wound.

The highest gifts of all are understanding of the things of faith, which objectively adds nothing to faith but is a sharper sense of faith, and wisdom, which feeds on the things of faith and, by their power, orders all things. This supernatural insight, this loving and sovereign knowledge should be the artist's spiritual light which gives him a heightened perception and enjoyment. With wisdom we link the serenity of the peacemaker's pure heart, which is always perceptible in the Christian artist's work. This is the peace and tranquillity of the divine order, connoting purity, integrity, and a complete absence of compromise. It is essential to religious art, of which one aspect must be that intangible, inviolable quality which, as Père Doncœur says, refuses to be drawn into argument.[28] And peace, the supreme beatitude, is the ideal of all religious works, as the Church sings in the hymn of dedication: *Cœlestis urbs Jerusalem, beata pacis visio*—blessed vision of peace, Jerusalem, the city of heaven.

[28] Père Paul Doncœur, *Péguy, la Révolution et le Sacré* (1941), p. 59.

Fortunately we do not have to rely on our imagination in order to know what the arts would be like if they were filled with the spirit of Our Lady. We know it already in Chartres, in the paintings of Fra Angelico, and in so many Romanesque churches and cloisters which testify to the miracles of love she has inspired in the artist's mind. Art must be virile, but since Our Lord, "the son of a woman," is responsible for all the best in us, there is obviously a special place for Mary in our lives. It is the place that God has given her, raising her up to the highest possible dignity. When Mary reigns over the arts of mankind, there is no place in our works for the harsh, bitter, or discordant tones that we so often note there.

In her are identified virginal purity and the supreme fullness of motherhood, and this is precisely the wonderful fusion we find in the works I have just mentioned. The tourist will never judge the façade of Chartres a miracle: the carved columns of the Portail Royal, the Baptist on the north door, the St. Gregory on the south door are so humble in their perfection that they give one the impression that their power over us is due to their modesty and retirement. The delight that they give us, likewise, is due to some gratuitous gift this sculpture possesses in virtue of the humility and purity of its aim and composition. This is how Mary took refuge in her lowliness and why God exalted her higher than heaven itself. Being the perfect virgin, she was worthy of becoming the Mother of God. The work of art conceived in this matrix, without any vain self-satisfaction on the part of the artist, is given the crowning glory, a deep, spiritual richness that communicates itself to the beholder. People come to Chartres because they have heard so much about it, and in reaction to this fame they tend to be prepared for a disappointment. But there is more than charm for them when they come—there is grace. How many people have visited Chartres out of curiosity, and been so overcome by peace and pure beauty that they have gone to confession, there and then to rid themselves perhaps of a lifetime burden of disquiet.

Mary is our mother because she is the Mother of God. She nurtures grace in our souls, and when she looks after our arts she teaches us to make them very human but at the same time very sacred. As the only mother who was ever justified in worshiping her son, she invites us to join her in adoration. She teaches us that supernatural tact which turns even our play, our amusement, and every graceful human act into something ennobling. God is not to be feared when she offers him to us as her child, while she in her simplicity fits into her own divinely appointed part in our salvation without the least ceremony or fuss. She simply contemplates in her child the Lord of Hosts. She has received from God the great dignity of true humility, which she has passed on to so many peasant women and which we need to beg her to bring into our art. She keeps everything that belongs to God in her heart, with infinite respect and silence, so that she cannot countenance the hasty, the superficial, the merely worldly, whether it be refined eighteenth-century worldliness or the vulgarity of our present age. All these obscure our feeling for what is divine, and so she will have none of them. Mary calls all artists to find their inspiration in the gentle, undisturbed contemplation which is her own.

She is the Mother of God, with the task of giving God that flesh which enabled him to suffer for our sakes. She is thus essentially the mother of sorrows, and since her suffering was borne that we might be taken out of our wretchedness, she is also the mother of mercy. An art which has learned Mary's lesson come from the heart and goes straight to the heart of the beholder. It bears the mark of that courage and restraint which were Mary's as she stood at the cross—and such an art is no stranger to tears.

The mystery is basically one of purity. Whereas the purity of Narcissus cuts us off from men, Mary's purity means forgetfulness of self, because it gives God priority over all things. Since she is the Immaculate Conception, exempt from original sin, she has no trace in her of that malice which encourages us to think of God's gifts as our own or to become complacent in the possession of them. Inevitably, the field of art is the one in which man is most prone to this form of pride, simply because the exaltation of the self is both a necessary cause and an effect of artistic creation. Since the fall, no one can be wholly disinterested in his work. The wounds that original sin made in our nature will only be completely healed in heaven, and so in this life even a saint is likely to find a little too much self-satisfaction in his own works. The artist, moreover, can be creating in order to make his enjoyment of himself as subtle and as intense as possible, even without reaching the extreme of what we might call artistic immorality, which is the enjoyment and exploitation in art of what is most perverse in the artist's soul. Gide's observation is unfortunately true: that every work of art is attended by three concupiscences, the lust of the eyes, the lust of the flesh, and the pride of life. The pride of life above all.

But Mary can say in truth that her works are "for the King," and this is the way in which all great works come about. We find our life when we have lost it and do not regret the loss. We receive hundredfold when we have given up everything to follow Jesus. Mary holds the secret for us. Like her, we must have perfect purity of heart, despising nothing, respecting everything as God's gift, giving him everything we have, and never seeking our own satisfaction in anything. Mary's center of interest is outside herself. No work of art can be achieved unless the artist transcends it.

3

LITURGY AND ART

What the Church is to her children, the liturgy must be to the artist who is trying to produce a sacred work. As soon as we raise any question regarding the function of religious art, it becomes evident that the liturgy must show us the direction to follow. At the moment, unfortunately, this seemingly obvious fact is often obscured, for many churches and their decoration are often not suitable for liturgical worship. What is even more regrettable is that we have overlooked the primary fact that the genuinely sacred character of a work of art is dependent on the part the liturgy has played in its conception in the artist's soul and creative imagination. What happens is that some people ignore the need for the inner discipline which must come from the liturgical life, while others demand that the artist be forced to conform to a certain style which is claimed to be "liturgical" instead of being invited to produce spontaneously what the liturgy brings out in him.

The second error, the most damaging in the sphere of religious art, is particularly rife in ecclesiastical circles and in certain religious communities. Since the liturgy is strictly

prescribed in the rubrics, it is often argued that an artist
seeking to produce a work for liturgical use must also submit
his work to these prescriptions. One has only to visit religious houses where the liturgy is carried out with extreme
care or glance through certain liturgical publications in
order to find signs of an exclusive taste for some particular
form of art—the Byzantine, for instance, the Romanesque,
or the Gothic, or certain recurring symbols like the peacock
and the dove. Obviously these symbols are vitally necessary,
but when they are used *ad nauseam*, they inevitably give the
impression of a fossilized religion which has been reduced
to a few formulas.

One's response to the liturgy must certainly be more
flexible than this, for the liturgy has taken on many different
forms in times past and will doubtless continue to do so in
the future. We should be able to distinguish what we may
freely adapt, what initiative we may take, from what is
essentially unchangeable. And if one can observe developments and changes in the essentials of the liturgy, it follows
that one should be able to find the same thing in less essential things, as for instance in the art forms which express the
true vitality of the liturgy. For the arts do precisely this.
They translate the mysteries which the liturgy celebrates
into a language that our feelings can grasp. They must be
thoroughly imbued with the mysterious character of the
liturgy, thus directing our minds beyond the sphere of appearances, but they must remain always on their own special level, which is that of our feelings. Anything rigidly
conventional and formal as regards style, or even merely

routine symbolism, can only falsify the liturgy and give it an effect of sterility and thus of uselessness in our lives.

The reason for regulating the ritual and the words of the liturgy was obviously so that the ministers celebrating the liturgy would be in agreement about what they were doing as they took part in the ceremonies. But this reason has no validity at all for the artist. The fixed formula for the celebration of the eucharist was designed to show how, by constant repetition of the same act, eternity was present in time and time in eternity. If vital words need repetition to achieve this effect, works of art which survive generation after generation are in themselves witnesses to a constant renewal of the spirit. Each one sings a new song. What best evokes the eternal is not reassessment but a constantly fresh response on the part of the creative spirit.

If the liturgy demands the preaching of the spoken word, it is precisely so that the sacred mysteries will be illustrated by language, so that what otherwise might remain stereotyped symbolism may be brought into conformity with the mentality of those who are called upon to share in it. Similarly, the silent preaching of architecture, painting, and sculpture must conform to the needs of the liturgy, while remaining free in its means of expression.

The more vital ritual and words are in the liturgy, the more they must be repeated for our benefit. That is why we could not bear to celebrate daily the feast of St. Cucuphas, let us say, whereas the *Pater noster* is new at every mass. There is always bound to be some temptation to routine and rote in the liturgy, but these prayers are so essentially

connected with the mysteries they adorn that on the whole
their repetition does us more good than harm. Art is different. It absolutely demands a constant renewal for its creative inspiration. We who behold works of art never tire
of those that are truly living and functional, whereas we can
never summon up any interest in the mass reproduction of
things we already know too well. For very good reason, the
liturgy should not be forced into the mold of any one religious style. But how often do we tend in practice to find
priests who imagine that a "liturgical" altar must have on it
squat little candles in squat little candlesticks, while they
condemn as unsuitable (because "unliturgical") the noble
and graceful workmanship of an earlier period. They demand columns on the side of the altar as liturgically essential, when these may only ruin an ensemble which is already
satisfactory in itself. They hack down superb retables to
"liturgical" proportions. Frequently these petty alterations
strike so false a note that the dignity of the liturgical sacrifice necessarily suffers from them, whereas the original ensemble may have been admirably fitted for its task. The
altar in question might have been lacking in certain desirable
features—the crucifix was perhaps not sufficiently imposing,
or there were too many secondary and distracting devotional
objects, or the altar table possibly was dwarfed by its ac-
cessories; but at least there was harmony, so that the whole
was uplifting to the faithful who worshiped there.

At the opposite pole from the "liturgical" obsession, we
find the viewpoint that the liturgy should give no directives
at all in the sphere of art. Usually this viewpoint arises be-

cause the liturgy is regarded only as a ritualistic element to be contended with. Those who so regard it have only seen it interfering with the arts and giving them a false expression. But they probably make this judgment because they are a shade too individualistic to embrace the mystery which the Church celebrates. They have not perceived the deeper meaning of the liturgy. It requires a certain enlightenment to realize that our salvation is the liturgical mystery, and that in consequence art can only find its meaning in relationship to the liturgy.

Fortunately, it is possible to dispel some of the more obvious misapprehensions, since there has been a widespread revival of interest in the liturgy. One can begin to see what art could be if it were once again to take its chief inspiration from the liturgy. It is not that the liturgy has lost any of its divine sublimity, or any of that extension which is manifest in the fact that Christ's presence is always renewed in the unfolding and passing of time. It is rather a loss of depth, a dimension that lies in the hearts of Christians, and this depth is bound to disappear when Christians lose their love of the liturgy. It is also to some extent a loss of breadth, since the idea that the liturgy must take everything human to itself has likewise disappeared. The liturgy has been the province of pedants and the highly cultivated, who, at a few famous churches and abbeys, put their efforts to executing it with scrupulous care and attention to detail. But since the liturgy has been recognized as pastoral and mystical, it is once again in a position of prominence, where it is able, as the primary and essential art of worship, to regulate every lesser art form dedicated to the Church's use. When it is re-established as the prayer of the faithful par excellence, it is pastoral. When it can give us an experience of its divine content, transcending all mere ritualism, it becomes once again mystical. In the words of Joseph Samson, "The divine life becomes human art."[1]

The purpose of the liturgy is to bring about a perpetual epiphany, for the liturgy can only be fulfilled in a visible form, and it can only be truly what it was meant to be when it unfolds as a thing of beauty. The unique thing about the liturgy is that it reconciles all our powers of sensitivity, knowledge, and love. It reconciles men among themselves and with God. The desire for harmony brings the arts into the service of the liturgy, all of them tending toward the beautiful, because they are concerned with order and proportion, with fullness and transcendence.

In its fullness, the liturgy gives the arts the necessary themes for their inspiration. It takes theology into the sphere of the heart and imagination, and transposes it into poetry, music, and drama. It speaks to the faithful without treating them as the "masses," awakening souls to the fact of their own inner secrets and opening minds to their heavenly Father and to their brethren. It develops a certain spirit in those who will take it as their guide—a *sensus Ecclesiae*, in its deepest meaning—because this is the way the Church understands the mysteries by which it lives.

The spirit alone can inspire the craftsmanship of an

[1] Joseph Samson, *Musique et Vie intérieure* (Paris: La Colombe, 1951), p. 234.

artist who wants to produce a sacred work. First of all, in a
very general way, it gives the artist the necessary perception
of the degree of autonomy that a work of art must have
with regard to the liturgy. There is nothing more odious
than the special intonation and way of speaking that some
priests use when preaching. But the word of God has a
special way of speaking and penetrating the soul of one in
communion with the faithful. The same affectation can
afflict the arts, when people self-consciously try to make art
"sacred." The liturgy offers the artist a spiritual discipline
by means of which his personality can be formed interiorly.[2]
When the artist produces a work designed for worship, it
will automatically have the tone or the atmosphere necessary for worship. But at the same time, as we shall see, art
brings into the liturgy things the liturgy cannot portray by
itself. This may be illustrated by an example.

It is true that the mass is the sacrifice of Calvary without
blood and without suffering. But in fact there is no blatant
evidence that the mass *is* the sacrifice of Jesus. Therefore,
if the altar crucifix is to be really liturgical, one might suppose that every sign of suffering, even of realism itself,
should be dismissed from the image of the Savior.[3] This is,
however, a naive supposition, for the fact that in the course
of time the cross with the figure on it has replaced the
originally bare cross indicates that the faithful have felt the
need to see Christ actually represented, offering his sacrifice
on the cross—to have their faith that the mass is invisibly

[2] *Ibid.,* p. 213.
[3] Pius XII in his encyclical *Mediator Dei* formally condemns this
view.

the sacrifice of Calvary thus confirmed. It is precisely because the mass is this invisible sacrifice that images are
desirable to make it to some degree visible. But this may
present another danger, since there is technically no limit to
which the principle of making up for the invisible by
perceptible means cannot be pushed. Since the means at the
disposal of artists must always be inadequate, it is impossible to lay down exact and precise rules. The only thing by
which the artist can be governed is the spirit of the liturgy
itself.

It is likewise impossible to define, except through this
spirit, the purely personal feeling and experience that can
be allowed in a work meant to help the devotion of the
whole community. The liturgy is fundamentally communal,
since it is the worship of God's assembled people, and the
arts are called upon to help unify this people. Many contemporary artists are intolerably self-revelatory, and it seems
utterly unjust that the personal idiosyncrasies of the individual should be inflicted in perpetuity on the faithful of
any particular church.

Against this, there is the unfortunate tendency to think
that, since the artist must bear all the faithful in mind, he
can only paint on a universal level. This is the approach of
the liturgy itself—impersonal and restrained—particularly
when it has something sad or moving to express. But in
fact the plastic arts need much more liberty of expression
than does the liturgy. The arts are meant to make explicit
the meanings that the liturgy holds in reserve. It is also a
mistake to suppose that in order to be universal one must
be impersonal, general, undifferentiated. Our aim should be

to disprove Nietzsche's assertion that every communion
tends to make us common, for the principle of our communion is transcendent, a communion of free persons, open
to the infinite. It must never be ruled by a common de-
nominator, lower than all the individuals concerned; it
must be ruled from above by something beyond all our different originalities, in virtue of the infinite which impels
each one of us.

What then is the difference between art which accepts
liturgical norms while exalting creative gifts and that which
is marked by too great an individualism? We can see the
difference in such a notable example as the Sistine Chapel,
between the vault and the far wall. The subjects are equal
in creative originality, but whereas everyone can accept the
great liturgy of the vault, many people are horrified by the
fact that the Christ of the Judgment is solely bent on rejecting the damned while Our Lady cringes behind him.
Admittedly, works of art are only great when the whole of
the creator's personality is involved in them, and it would
obviously be wrong if the liturgy prevented the full exercise
of any creative talent. But the creator's originality can unfortunately choose between following the *sensus Ecclesiae*
or disregarding it, can choose to give the results of a contemplation in which the most personal instincts are either
identified with the *sensus Ecclesiae* or are completely contrary to it. The frecoes of Tavant, the tympanum of Véze-
lay, the "Pietà of Avignon," the "Pentecost" of El Greco
are all works of intense individuality, but they are nonetheless universal in their appeal.

Any renaissance of the liturgy must essentially consist in an awakening of this *sensus Ecclesiae*, which we might consider fundamentally as a response to values. The strict observance of rubrics inevitably tends to make us think that they are all equally important, and this in turn helps us imperceptibly to forget the essential while we are busy with what is merely accidental. The obvious criterion of true value in the liturgy is *meaning*. The liturgy is a "forest of symbols" in which each reality is a symbol for something profoundly mysterious. Everything has reference to a higher, more sublime plane. Liturgical values are not of the allegorical order, that is, there is not a sign for each element signified. They are rather of the order of parable and apologue, possessing global meanings and reflecting the suppleness of nature itself.

The liturgical sense of values is, first of all, that feeling for Christ's glory of which we have already spoken. A church is an image of heaven. In the East, icons, mosaics, gold backgrounds, and groups of lamps all tend to produce the effect of an ecstasy, representing, as St. Simeon of Thessalonica says, "what is on earth, in heaven, and beyond heaven. The portico is the earth, the nave heaven, and the sanctuary what is higher even than heaven." The churches of the West have a similar symbolism, as we can see in the rite for the consecration of a church. If we truly live by the liturgy, we live again the mysteries of Christ in the radiance of his glory.

A really successful renaissance of the liturgy would ultimately show in the appearance of our churches. The Lord's

day and the Lord's house would be seen as belonging to the
Lord of Glory, risen from the dead, which would do away
with the lopsided modern emphasis on the somber tragedy
of Christ's passion. The fully developed liturgical life
teaches that the sacred arts must be inspired by a contemplation of the triumphant Christ. This liturgical atmosphere
is what we experience in St. Paul's letters to the Ephesians,
Philippians, and Colossians. Still less must the sacred arts
deal with our own fears. The excessive realism condemned
by Pius XII in *Mediator Dei* means, among other things,
any crude, bitter exaggeration of what is least appealing in
humanity, with no attempt at transfiguration.

Finally, the liturgy must develop the collaboration of
mind and emotions. Claudel, in an unforgettable phrase,
summed up the decline of sacred art as "the divorce which
has come about during the past century between the propositions of faith and the artist's powers of imagination and
feeling."[4] The decline of the liturgy came about as the result of a state of mind which was moralistic rather than
theological and mystical, individualistic rather than social,
and rooted in a Stoic or Cartesian conception of man rather
than in the traditional conception that we find in Aristotle
and St. Thomas.

When reason and will dominate the emotions, they engender a systematic religion which prescribes rules for vir-
tuous conduct and which is nurtured by "exercises of piety"
rather than by liturgical chant, gesture, and drama. Art can

----

[4] Paul Claudel, letter to Alex. Cingra, in *Positions et Propositions*,
vol. II.

only be reintegrated into our religious life and ritual can only regain its lost usefulness when our imaginations, our emotions, and our bodies themselves are given the place that belongs to them in the life of the whole person. We must remember, of course, that we are *rational* animals, however unattractive the thought may be to some of us. If we remember this, the arts will speak directly to the mind, reminding us of the truths of faith; works of art will be easier to understand. And at the same time, we shall have to try to be angels, insofar as we may, so as to give full scope to whatever in us has the power of taking wing. We shall not refuse to consider a work of art for which we can find no rational explanation, because we shall find that it invites us, as so much of our medieval heritage does, to a kind of global contemplation. Such a work may be enigmatic, but it will nevertheless possess a wealth of evocations and meanings for our souls. The "fine point of the soul," as St. Francis de Sales called it, makes a more immediate contact with the heart and feelings than it does with discursive reason. Religious art, like liturgy itself, will never mortify *anima* in order to please *animus*.

When we live by the liturgy, we are living by the spirit that breathes through Holy Scripture, the spirit of the Church, of which liturgy is the prayer. It is the Spirit of God that we live by, and our art must radiate the beatitudes of his Spirit. And since the Spirit of God is not exclusively confined to the sphere of art, no style need be laid down as essentially of this Spirit, which can breathe life into an infinite variety of forms. But if God's Spirit dictates no

specific form to the artist, it does bestow on him a very
sure and subtle discernment, which is our criterion of the
sacred and Christian value of the artists who live by the
Spirit.

4

ART AND TRADITION

If art is to be really sacred, it must be traditional. This is
the accepted teaching of the Church, which is made apparent in various points of positive law.[1] But whereas for a
Giotto or a Cavallini tradition came through their predecessors, one of the greatest problems in our time is that
a genuine tradition of sacred art seems to be lacking.

Today, individualism radically opposes all tradition. The
individual is a closed entity, unlike the person, who is open
to contact with the outside world. When we feel the need
to assert our autonomy in the face of laws which militate
against it (notably in the name of tradition), we are bound
to admit that we must, if we desire to be fully integrated
persons, depend on the rest of society in an infinity of ways.
It is a dependence through which we become fully conscious
that human nature implies a need for community and certain temporal limitations. We realize that there is an
enormous collective achievement which is prior to our
birth as individuals. We realize too that we are ourselves

[1] See the Holy Office Instruction on Sacred Art, Rome, June 30,
1952. These prescriptions are dealt with in Chapter 6, "The Laws of
the Church."

contributing to this collective achievement, and that we
are receiving from it, for the fulfillment of our personality,
far more than we could ever attain in isolation. And so we
discover tradition in the widest sense, as the incarnation of
the human spirit in human work—permanent, living, always renewed, constantly recognized by passing generations
as the heritage of all mankind. We become ourselves, the
more we share in this common patrimony.

Although the individual is conscious of an opposition to
tradition, there is in fact a close connection between his personality and what he can gain from the rest of mankind.
It becames obvious that our criterion for judging the value
of tradition is to be determined not only by human nature
but also by the capacity that tradition has for fulfilling
the personality. Something has obviously gone wrong with
tradition if it quenches the spark of the human spirit instead of stimulating it. Tradition is ideally an aid to freedom
and creativeness. But it is not surprising if tradition is misunderstood and misrepresented in our time, for the same is
equally true of the human person, whether as an individual
or in the mass of humanity.

If today the individual turns against tradition, he cannot
be wholly blamed, for tradition seems to be singularly
lacking in any sort of substance. For Giotto, a new world
was revealed by a host of traditions other than the one he
inherited immediately, but nonetheless this one remained
the tradition for him; having little knowledge of history, he
lived entirely in the present. But for us, history has made
the past an integral dimension of our present time. Tradition has ceased to be timeless. Instead of being for us a

stable permanent thing over the ages, it is very much a victim of the ravages of time. We can no longer confuse tradition with any one particular form it has adopted in the past, for we know now that these were all relative. On the other hand, it is an enormously difficult enterprise to disentangle tradition from these various forms. Above all, we have to distinguish tradition from the forms in which it supposedly appears in our own time, for these forms only discredit all the values tradition transmits to us from the past. They are the very worst superficial adaptations of the mode of yesterday. In this age of revolution, our pseudo-past is only a mockery when it attempts to help us find our true tradition.

Catholic tradition is not to be confused with any of the conciliar or patristic statements, major doctrinal currents, or monuments which have been its testimony throughout the ages. These things help us know tradition, and they deserve our respect on this account. But tradition is still something over and above them, since it is, as Möhler said, "the expression of the Holy Spirit breathing his life through the community of the faithful."[2] It is the Church in its profoundest manifestation. This is because the Word of Life, the Truth in person,[3] has come into time[4] and will remain until the end of the world.[5] The Word guides the

[2] Johann Adam Möhler, *Symbolik oder Darstellung der dogmatischen Gegansätze der Katholiken und Protestanten* (Tübingen, 1832), para. 28.
[3] I John 1:1, John 14:6.
[4] John 1:14, I John 1:2.
[5] Matt. 28:20.

Church by means of his Spirit along the way of truth,[6] teaching it all that he left in his message to the disciples.[7] It is not enough to conceive the Church's tradition as if it were a horizontal line, comprising yesterday, today, tomorrow, and all time.[8] We must see it rather as a vertical line that plunges to the depths of the mystery of God, living and working in his Church.

If we affirm that there is a tradition in the Church, we are claiming that the Church is always the same, despite all the superficial changes in its history. Tradition is the memory, in the Augustinian sense of *memoria*, of the Church. It is the permanence of the personality, always identical with itself, in the passing ages through which it lives. When we apply this view to the arts, we can see that tradition must be the vital principle by virtue of which they manifest the homogeneity of their development in time (thus proving the unity of the principle) and their diversity of expression (for which the fertility of the principle is, of course, responsible).

An acute consciousness of the relativity of art forms is something that helps enormously in our appreciation of tradition, for it makes us see how wrong it would be to identify tradition with any historical phenomenon. This error is the root of that "archeologism" which Pius XII condemned.[9] The fact that an art form belongs to one of the golden ages of the past does not give it the authority of

---

[6] John 16:13.
[7] John 14:26.
[8] Heb. 13:8.
[9] Encyclical *Mediator Dei*.

tradition, although it is a common misapprehension among artists that it does.

In the eyes of some, the fact that an art form is extant in our own day is enough to make it "traditional"—for instance, the exaggerated importance given the stations of the cross in our churches is labeled traditional, though this "tradition" dates back less than a century.[10] Criticism of the church's tradition is particularly valuable in relation to such supposedly traditional customs, for without it they might harden into an ineffaceable mask over the Church's face.

A particularly dangerous error, which includes all our previous examples, lies in limiting the life of the Church to the forms which it has hitherto shown. While tradition turns our eyes to the past, since revelation ceased with the death of the last apostle, it also looks to the future, since it is certainly far from having exposed its full deposit.

For over a century some religious artists, perplexed by the absence of a valid artistic tradition, have thought to rediscover the necessary norm of religious art in a previous century. Examples of this may be seen in the Gothic revival and in today's neoprimitives. But we have only to compare the original and its imitation to see how genuine feeling

[10] This is a typical deviation. I would be glad to know of any certain evidence for the existence of stations of the cross *inside* a church before the middle of the nineteenth century. The Abbé Hurel, in his book on Christian art (1868), speaks with regret of the introduction of stations of the cross into the church, which he says dates no further back than ten years. The way of the cross is a sorrowful devotion, and the church is a figure of the heavenly Jerusalem. It is a private devotion, and the church is designed for public worship.

has been blotted out and standardized. A "tradition" which produces dead works is not worth rediscovery; far from offering a valid norm, it dries up all creative endeavor.

Tradition is a constant, and beneath the infinite variety of forms offered by the sacred arts, the most obvious constant is the perpetual renewal of the creative process. Vulgar conventions and formulas of thought and style, which restore the dead letter without the spirit, only reveal more clearly, by contrast, that the action of real genius is like the divine act in its vitality.

After all, what is the use of having a tradition in sacred art in the context of time and according to the modes of art unless it allows us to share in the supertemporal Reality? Because that Reality is the three Persons of the blessed Trinity, tradition in art must foster the personal relationship between men and God. It must exalt the person both of the artist and of the observer. And since God is life, this tradition can only reveal itself insofar as it tends to bring things to life. Since God is eternally present, tradition, far from being tied to any reconstruction of the past, must take us into the very heart of our own present day. Tradition is only legitimate in art if it can be accepted by an artist worthy of the name, an artist like Jean Bazaine, for instance, who says, "There is only one absolute rule, and that is that every new work of art must be a fresh beginning."[11]

All art is fundamentally sacred, but the sacred quality has always to be directed in a certain way. If the sacred character is to be a Christian one, the artist's orientation must be

[11] Jean Bazaine, *Notes sur la Peinture d'Aujourd'hui* (Paris: Fleury, 1948), p. 35.

purified and supernaturalized; if the work of art is to speak the language of the faithful, the artist must be familiar with the life of the Christian community. These are the ways in which tradition is necessary to the artist. Left to his own devices, the artist will be far too vague in what he expresses, or he may err in apprehending what is sacred in the Christian sense. The artist does not have in himself that principle of divinization which will make his work perfectly Christian. The Promethean mentality maintains that man has a sort of divine spark by means of which he can reach God through his own efforts. This is indeed so common a view that many artists conceive that the creative urge is sufficient in itself, and that no correction of their ideas from the Church's tradition is necessary. But certainly no true Christian can accept the view that the creative instinct is sufficient to produce true Christian art without being supernaturally informed.

At the moment we are oscillating between false traditions which are repugnant to true genius and the hazardous life of that genius which lacks the direction of any authorized guidance. Tradition in sacred art can be found only — when we translate into art the tradition of the Church, while accepting the fact that the first artistic consideration is creative liberty.

But as I said, however confused our present situation may be, it does at least have the advantage of making it impossible for us to confuse the Church's tradition with all the pseudo-traditions of our time. An artist can find the essential in the tradition of sacred art when he accepts the Church's tradition, and this means living the life of the

Church, praying as the Church prays, receiving the sacraments, realizing to the full what membership in the Mystical Body means. Only then can we ever see tradition as a concrete and living reality which embodies truths. Just as a body can exist in a solid or liquid state, these supernatural realities, lived as prayer, a way of life, sacraments, can eventually be infallibly defined in dogmatic formulas by the magisterium of the Church. The actions which result from the application of these formulas to life embody these truths in a new and different way. Truly, one never ceases to marvel at the life of the Church, which is so complex and so exalted that its developments can never be reduced to any scheme, can never be limited in their possibilities by what has already been achieved. The life of the Church is always ready with new surprises for us, for sacred tradition is a living principle.

When we ask ourselves what tradition becomes when it is embodied in art, we must remember that it is never a substitute for talent or genius. The intuitions of a non-Christian genius can often be more profound and more productive than those of the artist who lives by the faith but who is less gifted artistically. But this truth must not be allowed to overshadow the fact that what is sacred in the Church must normally proceed from a man in whom the Church's tradition is living, who lives by sacramental realities with his whole heart and mind and even with his subconscious and in the Church's liturgy and according to her discipline. In the Byzantine world, the artist in the service of the Church was considered a consecrated person, much like a priest. Abbot Suger, writing in the twelfth century about the church he had decorated, quoted St. Paul's words, "All our sufficiency comes from God," and finished with the words, "The identity of the creator and his work brings about the sufficiency of the craftsman."[12] For he understood that if one wishes to build a church, one must oneself be built by the Church of God. Fra Angelico, who said that one must live with Christ if one would paint the things of Christ, could only conceive "life with Christ" along the traditional lines laid down by the practice of the Church. These three examples are sufficient to show us the line of our tradition, in which the sacred quality of a work of art is simply the mark of its creator's mode of being. To be sacred in the Church means to be sacred under the more or less visible influence of the Church. The normal way for this influence to manifest itself is by means of the traditional institutions of the Church. The Church alone can guarantee that the artist's inspiration will be full and firmly balanced, that it will flourish in the spiritual climate whch corresponds to it, and that it will give the feeling for the divine its true exaltation and human feelings their due limitation. This is the conclusion we reached when we were considering the liturgy, which is the most vital form that tradition makes use of to inspire the artist.

Tradition can only be translated into this spirit, into this feeling that an artist receives when, either in the Church or under its influence, he faithfully goes back to the main sources of inspiration. The artist need only open his mind

[12] Abbot Suger, P. L. 186; tr. Dom Leclercq (La Clarté-Dieu series, 18), p. 33.

to receive all that the sources—the word of God, the liturgy, the teaching of the great doctors of the Church, the living magisterium, the life of grace in holy souls—have to give.

Perhaps one can go further and suggest that the Church's artistic tradition is more than a spirit or a culture, for one can discover certain constant features in the discipline of the artist and in the means his art employs. First of all, there is the artist's dependence on the teaching authorities in the Church, the bishops, and on the priests who share in the episcopal activity. The Second Council of Nicaea decreed as a disciplinary measure that "the composition of religious pictures is not to be left to the initiative of artists, but is to be laid down by the principles of the Catholic Church and the tradition of religion. . . . Art belongs to the artist, and the composition of the picture belongs to the Fathers."

In the eighth century, the artist was an artisan, faithfully executing the composition stipulated by the clergy. But today art is invention, and the composition and organization of subject matter cannot possibly be taken away from the artist. This is why it is more than ever necessary that the artist be fully informed by the Church, and in this matter the clergy are the ones to provide the instruction. This implies in turn a close friendship between the artist and the priest. The clergy must not be authoritarian, but must translate for the artist of today the principles by which the Fathers lived. They should not compose the artist's picture for him, but they must open to him the whole world of Christian iconography, and point out that although the many vicissitudes through which it has passed give the impression that there is nothing there sufficiently stable to provide a norm, there are nevertheless dominant features and definite obligations to be derived from such a study. It has always been necessary, for instance, to give first place in the decorative scheme to the crucifix rather than to any other pictures or statues, even of the Sacred Heart. It is forbidden to portray Christ on the cross in such a state of abjection that nothing of his triumph is allowed to shine through. Similarly, the sanctuary is meant to evoke the eternal triumph and glory of Christ in a way which is both majestic and serene. Among the dominant characteristics of Christian iconography one must insist on the Church's preference for facts, for those facts that the liturgy celebrates symbolically.

There is a definite tradition in Christian icongraphy by means of which theologians and art historians can convey the sacred symbols of Christianity in all their complexity and subtlety to the artist of our time. Unfortunately, many people tend to be too rigid and systematic in what they understand by iconography. Some will ally themselves exclusively with Roman antiquity, others with Byzantium, still others with the Romanesque or the French styles of the thirteenth century. These tight compartments are a joy to those who like a narrowly limited world, but they discredit iconography in the eyes of living artists, who are not looking for a system and who need simply to be given fresh and vital ideas for inspiration.

Christian tradition in sacred art can be a living discipline for the artist, provided he does not approach it as too specialized a regimen. Retirement from the world is even more dangerous to artistic creation than to the spiritual life.

Whoever has had some experience of monastic life knows
very well (if, as a Christian should, he preserves his free
judgment) the risks that this retirement brings. For retirement should make one remote from the society of men only
as regards the world, the flesh, and the devil (in the Johan-
nine sense); this withdrawal should bring about an even
deeper communion with one's fellow men. But far too many
overdo this separation from the world of men so that they
become Pharisees. Instead of charity and the beatitudes, they
are exclusively preoccupied with completely irrelevant concerns peculiar to their own religious communities. Similarly, the artist, if he is to produce a sacred work, must find
a suitable environment in which to live with Christ. But if
he is to keep in real contact with the world, as he must, it is
imperative that this environment be not too restricting
either psychologically or materially. Whatever comes down
to us in our tradition as an echo from the past must be
transposed according to the conditions and circumstances of
the artist of our time. It would be fatal to prescribe any
mystique of sacred art that might claim to fix the rules of
art rigidly.

"A painter must work with his whole soul. His heart must
be at peace, and it must be absolutely pure and sincere."[13]
This Chinese maxim reminds the artist of his need for recollection and contemplation, for prayer and gentleness and
goodness. There must always be communion with nature—
not of a pantheistic sort, obviously, yet nonetheless "in
harmony with the rhythm of the cosmos," which is the

---

[13] Chinese texts quoted by Oswald Siren, in *Bulletin de l'Associa-
tion française des Amis de l'Orient*, April, 1934, pp. 28–29.

first rule of the Tao in painting. A sense of this rhythm is usually innate, but it can be cultivated. A harmony between the inner world, which creation both conceals and reveals, and the world of love in which the artist must dwell, a harmony between himself and his faith, and a harmony between himself and all men—these form the decisive experiences which are the source of any truly sacred work of art. It was for this purpose that Fra Angelico demanded "more calm" in the artist's life, with a view to "living with Christ." Here we are at the very heart of tradition in sacred art. Without this essential harmony all the conventions and rules are worthless. The artist must create this harmonious atmosphere, perhaps in family life, perhaps in a community of fellow artists, perhaps in a religious order, but it must be an atmosphere in which a pure Christian life may flourish, in which the artist may deepen his love while following faithfully the movement of inspiration.

The most important thing for an artist, to cite another Chinese painter, is for him to bear in his heart the reality he is trying to express.[14] And yet another asks, "What is painting? It means re-creating things in our minds according to the divine models, rendering them apparent by means of the brush."[15] This is very far removed from the practice of observing certain rules and composing according to the approved style, but it is in perfect accord with the mission of the Christian artist, whose task is to capture something of the shining radiance of Christ's glory. The "divine models," far from being any ideal figures handed down by

[14] Quoted in *ibid.*, p. 17.
[15] I thank Philippe Stern for this quotation from Ts'ien Ku.

tradition, are simply mysterious images which come from
the contemplation of a world illuminated by love and full
of revelation.

Tradition demands above all, then, that the artist be a
man who is body and soul in harmony with the rhythm of
nature throughout his life and in the production of his
work. He is meant to be familiar with these rhythms, and
to perceive in them the effects of the creative act of God.
His own acts, which must try to conform to the act of God,
thus have a contemplative aspect. The artist's work is an
initiation into mystery. It is sacrificial, for with the completion of any work, the worker consecrates to God and to his
brethren in God the mysterious operations of nature in
which the divine action is hidden. Then the work has a
sacred character, and it is capable of fulfilling a sacred function.

If I have introduced certain non-Christian maxims into
these considerations on tradition, it is only because in this
matter of the artist's discipline the tradition of Christ's
Church rejoins a human tradition that is older still. I am
not accepting a syncretism, but rather substituting for the
vague pantheism of the Tao the definite principles of the
Christian faith.[16] Christ is the center of our faith. We have
to bring to him everything which tends toward him in
humanity, and let it come into the orbit of his radiant glory.

[16] It is quite easy to accept the idea of communion with the
cosmos if one bears in mind St. Augustine's distinction between use
and enjoyment, and remembers that for a Christian this communion
cannot be a mere dissolution into the universe or a passive submission to its laws but must be a liturgical act which man celebrates
through the "priesthood" of his creature quality.

Christian faith, nurtured and defined by the Church's whole life, makes the necessary adjustments.

The artist's wisdom comes from a soul that is naturally Christian. It is not the same with symbols, which are often difficult to "baptize" for Christian use in mission countries. But this problem is not one that need concern us here. For the Western artist there is no problem if he simply translates the faith of the Church instead of speculating on what "primitive tradition" may have been. The simple rule he should follow is that there must be nothing in his art which requires an initiation different from the ordinary initiation which all the faithful receive in their baptism and Christian upbringing.[17]

[17] See my article "À la Recherche de la Tradition," *L'Art Sacré*, nos. 5–6 (1949).

5

The Idea of the Sacred Today

Society has lost much of its feeling for the sacred since the days of Hölderlin's *Hyperion*. If in our time we find a renewed awareness of the sacred, this is not to be attributed simply to a rebellion of the irrational instincts against the tyranny of reason. It corresponds to what André Malraux calls "the awakening of fatality"—the unleashing of forces which can be neither controlled nor judged at their true worth, and which have increased in the same measure as has the tyranny of reason. It is precisely the development of a civilization devoid of anything sacred that gives rise to a primitive passion for the sacred in many men today.

It is because we are moving so quickly that we are getting back to where we began. Man has once again become the plaything of the elements, and has acquired a new and basic respect for the crushing weight of destiny. He is full of superstition, full of naive wonderment when confronted with new marvels. He is an easy victim of collective fanaticism and panic. And all this is because man can glimpse a kind of transcendence in the elements of his destiny, which is something mysterious and often terrifying and yet filled with a great hope for some future salvation.

This new passion for the sacred can be recognized in various guises. It is particularly apparent in the present deeply felt need for integrity and purity. How to satisfy this need poses a great problem. We are told that only nothingness is pure. But the sense of the sacred which is born primarily of disgust results in a withdrawal into sterile solitude; it is the path of despair. But such a sense of the sacred can be healthy in that it implies a refusal to compromise, to accept whatever is not absolutely genuine. For many people, purity simply means detachment from material creation. Like the Manicheans of the Middle Ages, who were called Cathari because of their boasted purity, these people imagine that matter must be evil. Moreover, this attitude can often be a pretext, an excuse for impurity on the grounds that the flesh is too weak. But this misconception of purity and this fundamental Manichean error must not blind us to the excellence of true purity. As St. Dominic saw clearly, we can only conquer a wrongheaded and misguided conception of purity by an even greater, truer purity. This Manichean heresy is a common one, and Christians cannot compromise with it.

The kingdom of God is within us, and the qualities of the sacred must also be sought from within. Of course, this does not mean that we must exclude from our life what is objectively sacred, such as sacraments, monuments, rites, and customs. On the contrary, our demand for the absolute should be all the stronger precisely because we are not Manichean but incarnate beings who are only too happy to mediate between the two worlds of body and spirit.

We should express our loving fidelity to this task by

showing respect to all created things. And the more we live according to this conviction, the more we shall realize that created things have a spiritual quality corresponding to the sacred character imparted to them by their liturgical use.

A religion that is reduced to mere ritualism regards a church, a sacred vessel, a liturgical ceremony as sacred only because they have been validly consecrated; ritualism does not recognize the sacred quality imparted to them by the spiritual beauty which appeals through the senses to the soul. But where there is a real feeling for beauty, such ritualistic religion is bearable only through heroic faith.

All deviations from a true sense of the sacred may perhaps be traced to the irreducible part of human nature which is passion. Therein lodges the ultimate redoubt of the sacred, the *nescio quid horrendum* which cries out to be satisfied. This, together with our irrational drives, is the remnant of transcendence in a soul which has rejected both God and the world and which creates its own gods within the obscure forces of the soul. Understood this way, the sacred is a revolt. It is the unchaining of the passions, not for the sake of purposeful activity but simply for destruction, even the destruction of those very powers which have been unleashed. The sacred is thus conceived as a fundamentally destructive force with one outlet in crime, another in carnal pleasure, and yet another in the constant pursuit of that magic moment of complete fulfillment when one has the feeling of being released into some higher state. There is a great difference between the spiritual experience that siezes what is eternal in the present moment and the experience that exalts what is only perishable and transitory in that moment. In the first case beauty, the aura of poetry or song, in brief some fullness of experience comes as a reward; in the other case, these rewards are pursued as ends in themselves. But the sacred is sufficiently ambiguous to prevent us from determining exactly which of these two we are in the presence of. Only God can judge this. The true and the false are bound to be almost indistinguishable from each another, for only the transcendent is completely at home in the transcendental order. The great problem is to know whether the sacred, in any work of art, is a communion with the living God or with primeval chaos.

It is the transcendent that engenders the sacred in art. Therefore, Christian worship above all should be stamped with the character of mystery. This is in contrast to past centuries, which sought either to subject the holy to rational analysis or else to reduce it to the level of the commonplace by obscuring it with sentiment. In our time, as the faithful become more and more aware of the God of the Bible and of the *Te Deum*, they tend to lose interest both in theodicy and in saccharin devotions.

The liturgy (when properly celebrated) has once again become the sincerest expression of our feeling for the sacred. The antithesis between the Christian and the sacred rite, between the Christian and the community, can only disappear through that love which at once animates the liturgical celebration and the faithful. In this experience, still not too common in our time but growing more frequent, we realize that Christian transcendence is in infinite love.

We discover in this way one of the ambivalences of the sacred. The need for asceticism, for the stripping of self, is allied to a radiation of spiritual splendor. They are correlative factors, two aspects of the same thing. There is the little bare chapel with its small handful of people, in a silence which is in perfect accord with the simplicity of the vestments, and the one small window over the altar, or it may be the Cathedral of Chartres, with eight thousand young people taking part in a dialogue mass; in either case there is the fullness of love. We need not think of the bare chapel as something Jansenist, and we need not think of liturgical splendor in terms of brocade and gilt and plush, orchestras and violins. Whether it be the sound of magnificent choirs and organs or a few voices in unison, the secret place of the heart is always opened to God's love.

The Christian's vocation is solemn and sacred. It is, as Malraux said, "destiny made individual."[1] which means not that Christian destiny is something blind, a mere fatality, but that the designs of a loving providence shape the Christian's liberty. The heart of man is more sacred than the temple, and the restoration of a sense of the sacred can only come about by the growth of holiness within the heart of the individual and throughout the Mystical Body of the community. Some groups of Christians, some parishes, live intensely by that mystery which one might call the interpenetration of society and person. This makes the primitive

[1] André Malraux, *Psychologie de l'Art*, II, 61.

experience of the sacred seem by comparison a trivial thing, as indeed it is, primarily because of the spiritual level on which Christian experience takes place and in particular because of the quality of love that the Christian experience engenders.

But this experience, which is indispensable if Christian art is to flourish, occurs frequently only in a few communities. There are thousands of Christians who very rarely undergo this experience. And this has an unfortunate effect on art, since in the order of art consecration is made apparent rather by the quality of plastic and pictorial form than by stylistic technique or by particular procedures or materials. But how can we agree on the quality of the forms involved unless there exists a common experience of love and of the sacred?

The temptation to reduce the Christian sense of the sacred to mere formalism is almost inevitable, for the simple reason that the Christian does not need to draw a line between what is sacred and what is not. Everything save sin is either sacred or capable of becoming sacred. Every rigid system of Christian art which claims to have its own consistency, its own laws and outlook, inevitably formalizes the sacred. The same is true of all ritualism that is devoid of life and has become a sham. This is not really surprising, of course, since every sacred expression becomes ritualized, and sacred art has always involved (like any other application of art to a specific function) submission and recourse to conventions. The symbolism of Christian art needs a system and it must have its own laws. But the conventions governing the sacred must be genuine in three ways: first, these conventions must constitute a language as direct and as transparent as possible to express the things of God and to convey their full meaning; second, this language must be used sincerely by the best artists of the period; and third, it must be the sincere and habitual expression of the faith of Christian people.

If the conventions which we have recourse to in sacred art conform to this threefold standard of authenticity, we have no need to fear formalism; but if our conventions are adopted in a spirit of reaction, then we cannot expect them to be very fruitful. Nothing in Christianity can ever be fruitful unless it is done in the framework of our communion with mankind as it really is. We have to be on our guard against any sense of the sacred that prescribes a closed system of signs, divorced from the life of our age and condescending to the individual Christian as if it were the heavenly Jerusalem coming down. Every sacred work is something of an epiphany, a transfiguration and a *parousia*. But it is so only in terms of our present humble condition, in which we can do nothing of value for God if we are not in communion with each other. And what art is possible when we are as divided as we are today?

Finally, we have to remember that our sense of the sacred must always be a cosmic one, for all creation, the first sin of man nothwithstanding, is sacred. Man is no longer in agreement with creation, but that is because man, not crea-

tion, has sinned. Ideally, man should find his place in creation as in a temple. He is the celebrant of the liturgy of creation. It is he who must find its secret meaning, and fathom
each creature as a symbol of the Creator. In contemplating
creation, as St. Maximus says, man finds "the revelation of
Wisdom which is mysteriously hidden in the law."[2] He
gives creatures their mission, which is to serve God's glory
by filling some holy use. Everything is ours, as St. Paul
said, and we are Christ's, and Christ belongs to God.[3] The
"use" in question is the one which man attains by his own
creative work. By his "poetic" knowledge of things, he dis-
closes their secret and reveals their inner beauty. Through
the liturgy he brings all things to the great offering of
Christ to the Father.

Our day and age has seen the rediscovery of these things,
in poetry, in psychoanalysis, in the study of the Greek
patristic tradition and of the history of religions. Every
thinking person, whether or not he is aware of these things
specifically, must henceforth be aware of the sacred to the
degree that he is aware of the universe around him. This
awareness is much more important than the mere "feeling
for nature" of romantic literature, and it is of enormous
importance to sacred art.

"The soul that loves immortal goodness," said St. Cath-
erine of Siena, "reveres everything." Art that is imbued with
the Christian quality of seriousness will always have the
honest goodness of simple, wonderful things like bread,

[2] See Hans Urs von Balthasar, *Liturgie cosmique*, p. 230.
[3] I Cor. 3:23.

cheese and honey; the mysterious enchantment of ordinary
things is a great source of the sacred in art. There may be six
ceramic candlesticks on an altar, and yet no two will be
alike. Their symmetry is like that of plants that have been
cultivated or cut to look alike, but their very individuality
makes them different. The color of the ceramic is full of
variation, and to the eye has the freshness of young plants in
springtime.

Everything in human art is ready and waiting to be consecrated and to enter into the larger sphere of God's creation. The indefinable qualities of things that grow or are
freshly gathered have a parallel in the quality of man's creation that is the result of the love in the artist's head and
heart and hand. It resembles the spontaneous upsurge of
life, and as such is infinitely worthier of being given in
homage to God than any of the accepted pedantries of so-
called sacred art. The finest symbolism of all is that which
goes to the mind through the eye. The complications of
reason, the laborious efforts of memory, even if their objects
are theoretically nobler in themselves, have not the virtue of
spontaneous life and generation. The former make us think,
but they do not give us an experience of being born anew.

Perhaps the example I have taken is too simple, and
some will object that it is much more difficult to keep the
morning look of innocent freshness in a painting or a building or any complex work. Yes, I admit that, but at least we
can agree that it is essential to try to preserve it. Most artists
seem to be looking for something quite different. Neither
sad experience nor any amount of reflection or systematizing

need necessarily take away the freshness that belongs to the flowers in the dew. A child may look innocently at the world, but a saint, knowing all there is to know of the heart of man through his inner experience, can observe it even more innocently than a child. In all things, we must try to see the work that God has made.

6

THE LAWS OF THE CHURCH

The Church has recently given some very clear directives on the matter of sacred art. Without claiming to lay down the law completely, she has been led by various circumstances to enunciate certain obligations and prohibitions. There are still many points about which she has said nothing and possibly never will. Therefore, it would be wrong to construct any theory of sacred art on the basis of these laws, which concern only particularly vital points. It is obviously preferable to study the arts themselves, as we have been doing, so as to arrive at the laws as a verification of what the facts reveal.

Canon Law recognizes that art has laws of its own.[1] In other words, it does not consider sacred art as something which can be treated in an arbitrary manner. Positive prescriptions of Canon Law remain general, much to the distress of those who like to be told exactly what to do in every situation life can offer. But the Church here is only follow-

---

[1] Canon 1296, para. 3, distinguishes among "laws of sacred art," "liturgical prescriptions," and "ecclesiastical tradition." They can only be distinguished from the standpoint of art itself.

ing what we might call the law that directs all ecclesiastical laws, namely, grace itself. In the Church everything is prescribed with a view to the primacy of the spirit. The necessary element in all legislation is the ability to foresee excesses and to lay down conditions of life. Laws cannot themselves give that life, or predict how it will develop. When working for the Church, an artist often fears that his spontaneity may be crushed because he is now moving into a sphere governed by strange new laws which will dictate his every movement.

As a matter of fact, the demands of the liturgy do not lay down very many prohibitions or directives, and what may well escape the artist is that he is not really familiar with the positive realities involved. Rules and regulations are only dead letters until the artist has come to grips with what is real and positive in the domain of sacred art. An artist who can perceive, though only in theory, what are the realities involved will usually accept wholeheartedly all the legislation laid down; but if he cannot perceive them he may become obsessed with one rule alone and sacrifice all the rest.

The worst thing an artist can do, however, is to observe all the rules faithfully without embracing the spirit that gives them life. For example, we all know that there must be a crucifix on or above the altar. But the important point is that the artist discover why the Church has laid down this rule. When the artist knows that Christ on the cross is the only figure required on the altar, he will realize that it is meant to stand out as the object of most vital importance.

Yet all too often the mere letter of the law is observed by the inclusion of a tiny crucifix which is dwarfed by its surroundings.

If we understand the Church's laws properly, we will find that they never act as obstacles to the artist's free invention. Unfortunately, they have to be properly understood, and more often than not they are misunderstood. We find that many of the clergy see the Church's laws on sacred art as a narrow set of conventions, while some artists proclaim that there are certain types of constraint that are beneficial to art. In the 1920s, thanks to a number of pronouncements by Maurras and Gide, it was held that art lives on constraint and dies of too much liberty. Regrettably, no one bothered to ascertain what constraint and what liberty might be in question. It is true enough that the artist has to be tied in some way to his form, and the limitations of a given material may act as a stimulus for an artist of real talent. But the demands involved will differ from one case to another. Arbitrary conventions which have nothing to do with the particulars of a case would have the effect of stereotyping works of art and of sterilizing the inventiveness of a true creator. Above all, it would be wrong to enforce some stylistic formula which is quite irrelevant to the work that the artist is producing.

If any conventions are imposed they must be of a type to which the artist can spontaneously fit himself. And here there is no point in citing the case of Racine, who undoubtedly benefitted by the three unities and the Alexandrine, because these very features contributed to the rapid decline of the classical theater. From Racine onward, these conventions served only to inhibit a purer lyricism. Imagine what their effect would have been on a Claudel! One must ascertain first of all whether a constraint is of a type to hamper a work of art or to help it structurally. It is not enough to consider the rules of art as if they were the rules of a game which the artist willingly plays. They are much more. They are a vital principle of work and development in the artist. They must be so integrated as to be part of him, a part to which he conforms with ease and pleasure, as to the demands of his own nature. They must affect the exercise of his art at the level at which it is most personal to him.

If we understand the Church's positive laws and prohibitions as they are meant to be understood, we will find in them nothing that hampers the artist. On the contrary, they are extremely helpful. If certain people try to limit what the Church has said to some narrow interpretation, it is because they are trying to canonize their own conception of art. But the Church, being catholic, will never make any particular art form obligatory, for she is universal, in space, in time, and above all in her acceptance of everything contained in human nature. We shall find people who can only conceive of art as an *enfant terrible*, in constant need of a rigid discipline, without which it can do nothing but harm. This inevitably either has a sterilizing effect on art or reduces it to a state of servility in which no rich, spontaneous expression is possible but only a dreary conformity to some completely artificial program. Art cannot be treated as the slave (nor does the Church intend that it should be so treated) but as the very noble servant of the liturgy, whose sacred function exalts art's nobility all the more.

The Holy Office issued an instruction on June 30, 1952, in which the major texts on sacred art, from the Second Council of Nicaea to Pius XII, were summed up. The principal point made in this instruction is the one we have already discussed—the dependence of art on liturgy. The chief difficulty involved has two aspects: the obligation to observe "the forms received from Christian tradition" (Canon 1164, para. 1), and the prohibition of what is *insolitum*—unusual (Canon 1279, para. 1). On the face of it, it might seem that the Christian artist in the service of the liturgy is bound to copy the styles which were created in the Church during past periods when art was allowed to be inventive. But this is just another case where the terms involved only make sense when we have discovered what the facts are.

The Church's artistic tradition, as this instruction reminds us, is relative, varied, and constantly open to new ideas. All the doors must be left open, and the field must be a free one. The Church invites artists to absorb the spirit in which the works of the past were created and which still gives them life, and to discover in these works the laws of artistic creation which embody the Christian outlook. The Church reminds her artists that they cannot be mere innovators. They have to realize that they are continuing a tradition and are part of a continuity. She shows them what is the best milieu for them to flourish in.

There is a definite culture involved in sacred art which the artist must not only accept but also assimilate, so that it becomes part of his being. The fidelity we owe to the forms of the past demands that we take the art of the past, like the saints of the past, as our models. But instead of blindly copying them, we are called upon to correspond with our own special graces as they corresponded with theirs. Unfortunately, there is a stronger temptation to imitate repetitiously what is considered beautiful in the art of the past than to imitate what was thought remarkable in the lives of the saints. If we can speak of the materials of the art of sanctity, these must be the flesh that suffers, the soul that strives, the passions that rebel and must be trained. This asceticism is far less subject to obsolescence than are styles of painting or sculpture.

As regards the *insolitum*, the unusual, this again does not mean simply anything that the faithful have not become accustomed to. If it were so, it would mean the end of all artistic creation. We must define the unusual in terms of the faith. A picture must in no way upset the faith of Christians. The rule of faith implies here that everything in art must be avoided that could be an occasion for error on the part of the uneducated and uninstructed. But the unusual must also be thought of with regard to the emotions as well as to the faith of Christians. Certainly the Church has in mind the fact that what is unusual can upset people's feelings as well as their faith. There should be nothing shocking about works of art in churches. But does this mean that the Church disapproves of anything new because people are initially disturbed by it? Surely not. Anything that is "new" in matters of faith is bound to be a corruption, because we already have the total revelation made in the Church; but this cannot apply to art, in which the expression of the truths of faith is always new because human feelings vary

from generation to generation. Nor can we reason about
works of art in the Church as we may about customs, which
achieve the force of law when they have been established
long enough. Art, like the leaves that grow on trees and the
fruit produced in time by flowers, keeps its vigor only as
long as it is fresh and living. It would be wrong to accept
for church use only art which is, as it were, withered and
dry.

The unusual, then, can only be gauged in relation to the
esthetic outlook of a period. This means that one has to be
deeply conscious of the art being produced in any given
time. And it is also relative to the communities of Christians for whose contemplation the work of art is intended.
This is why the code of Canon Law requires that bishops
judge the suitability of works of art for the churches in their
dioceses. A work that could give scandal in Italy might not
do so in Germany or some other country. The chapel at
Vence is not at all unusual to the sisters for whom Matisse
designed it, whereas it would be in most parishes.

Some people will enjoy what appears to others as "de-
pravity" or "deformation" of wholesome art, deviations
which Pius XI made particular reference to in *Mediator Dei*
(Canon 1178). There are even those who have supposed
this condemnation to apply to Rouault! It is difficult, but
not impossible, to form an objective judgment on many
works of art. Far too many of these "deformations" and
"depravities" are perpetrated today in the name of sacred
art. Various things have been condemned in precise terms
—tabernacles without a completely enveloping veil, crosses
with the arms almost vertical, the Holy Trinity depicted as

three men sitting side by side, Our Lady in priestly vestments, Our Lord wearing a specific religious habit.

Some have even insisted that Pius XII also condemned nonobjective art in two texts referring to an excess of symbolism.[2] The Pope did indeed speak with regret about deviations in art which prevent it from serving as the international language that it should be. He spoke, for instance, of a lack of expressive value which makes the art work fail to convey the artist's thought or manifest his feeling. When a work of art needs a verbal commentary to be understood, it loses its significant value and becomes a mere pleasure for the eye, with nothing offered to the mind.

No one, however, has any right to claim that these texts exclude everything nonobjective. We are told plainly that exaggerated symbolism means that which requires some explanation external to the work itself. We are all too familiar with the sort of work that is overloaded with meaning and is nothing more or less than a puzzle to be unraveled by those whose curiosity is challenged. There are abstract paintings that show this fault, but more often than not the puzzle-pictures are representational. As regards the needs and demands of particular communities, experience has already proved that once they are accustomed to abstract work, they find it quite acceptable.

Nothing is so dreadful as the concentrated disapproval of those who erect hard and fast barriers between the acceptable and the unacceptable and who call down the wrath of

[2] Pope Pius XII, *Mediator Dei*, and his discourse to the congress of Catholic artists given in September, 1950, and printed in the original French in *L'Osservatore Romano*, September 6, 1950.

God on anyone who ventures into the places which they themselves have put out of bounds. What they are doing is completely opposed to the Church's principle of *odiosa sunt restringenda*, whereby anything which would seem to fall under an interdiction, without manifestly so falling, is to be given a liberal interpretation. In the question of what constitutes an excess of symbolism, the meaning of the texts is clear enough, and there is no need to stretch them to include certain spheres in which modern art is achieving its finest works and ministering well to the needs of Christian communities.

From this particular question we can even draw a conclusion for this chapter, and indeed for the whole of the first part of this book: there is nothing in the Church's laws on sacred art, if they are properly understood as the Church means them to be understood, which is opposed to an art that is truly sacred and truly alive. The restraining hand that the Church has laid, for instance, on excessive realism and excessive symbolism and the obligation she imposes of speaking a universal language and of satisfying the deepest needs of the faithful are the fundamental demands of all sacred art. Obviously, these formulas are not enough in themselves either to achieve what is desired or to eliminate abuses. But they do invite the creative artist to live a true interior life and to imbibe that Christian character of fundamental seriousness which is the principle of all sacred art.

But we must always guard against any pharisaical interpretation of the liturgical directives on sacred art which would engender a new academicism. The more pharisaical the interpretation becomes, the more we find art reduced to a mere conformity and to bad taste. There will always be a large number of mediocre artists who are only too happy to follow rules mechanically. It would be lamentable if they were allowed to block the paths of living art. We must take every care to see that nothing hampers either the lyrical quality of art or the creative genius which has so rarely appeared in sacred art since Tiepolo. This lyricism need in no way be hampered by the laws of the church if these are properly understood; indeed, it has everything to gain from them.

PART II

THE DEMANDS AND POTENTIALS
OF LIVING ART

7

THE LIFE AND QUALITY OF ART

Art, as Maritain said, has its seasons, like nature,[1] and only the Lord has the right to curse the barren fig tree in the season when no one would expect it to bear fruit.[2] Other trees at other times give other fruits, and these, because they come in due season, have their own particular value. But since the nineteenth century, people have refused to accept the fruit that the season offered, and have preferred to believe that the fruit of past seasons was still ripe.

It is very important to realize what direction art is taking today in relation to the sacred. We have to think of the demands of art as well as of its possibilities, both of which are often misunderstood. Most Catholics are not interested in what contemporary art has to offer, asking it instead to provide them with things it cannot possibly give any longer.

We are living in an age of spiritual poverty. The poor have their own special brand of wealth, but most people today have rich men's desires; they frustrate themselves by hankering after treasures of past ages which can never again

[1] In *Art and Scholasticism.*
[2] Mark 11:13.

be ours. They are not only asking for figs; they want literally everything that is out of season. Our age is one of general inflation. This we can see easily enough in the sphere of religious art. People want everything, whether or not they have any right to it and whether or not it is still available.

This brings us to the need for an examination of the present resources of art. In times past, there was more understanding and more contact between the artist and his public. Now we must learn to accept the disparity between what the people want and what the artists are able to give. The fundamental question is of the value and the quality of art; indeed, it is whether art exists at all, for it only exists insofar as it is genuine and of value. Artists today might well ask themselves the question, to be or not to be? This is something new in history that we must face. Before we ask ourselves what art is capable of giving us and what artists may be allowed to expect of it, we have to discover whether what we are talking about is art at all. All that is required in sacred art is that it have a sacred character, or rather, as I said before, that it simply have character. We cannot talk about the religious quality of works of art, the spiritual tendencies and intentions of artists, unless the works in question have some quality.

Our age has been obliged to coin the phrase *living art*, a pleonasm which implies that we have with us a large quantity of "dead" art. Popular art has almost entirely disappeared from the town and country districts where not so long ago we found such charming works on a humble scale. The artists who created them were gifted with a real sensitivity which has since atrophied. The ideal of artisans today is to imitate the expressionlessness of machinery. The feeling for forms and materials has been lost, together with simplicity. Similarly, architecture has become more and more ugly during the last century as it has aspired more and more to being beautiful. The restorers of ancient buildings have been largely unconscious of the magnificent qualities of these structures, so that the coarseness and lack of understanding of their restorations often make us wince. If such renovators have so little feeling for existing forms, we should not be surprised that their own works and their own teaching are equally incompetent.

Further, there has not been one creative genius during the last century who has not been considered during his lifetime either a madman or a charlatan. Twenty or forty years after their deaths, they have, of course, been recognized as great masters. Thus the public of today, and those who are responsible for forming its opinions, have been conditioned in their ideas by people who have proved themselves incapable of appreciating their own contemporaries. Is it likely, then, that we are in a better position to judge the work of the artists of our time?

All these things have so infected the arts as to give the impression of a kind of original sin. This phenomenon is another sign of the general lack of harmony in the very depths of the human psyche that characterizes our time. The man of today has lost that unity of spirit in which the feelings are more intuitive than reflective. Now we find him rejecting his intuitions and relying more on his reasoning powers, while his ideas are all too hastily gathered and too easily systematized. In such a fundamental imbalance, the poetic feeling for life has suffered the most.

Popular art and the spontaneous good taste of the common man have been destroyed by three centuries of academicism. Together with this, an industrial regime has been imposed on most of society, while the organization of national life has become more elaborate and ponderous. Every level of culture is bound to show the ravages of such a conglomeration of bad influences. It is no longer sufficient for us to contemplate beautiful things, for even our capacity to see has been injured. The combined effects of the industrial revolution and the academic outlook are something that can now be taken for granted in the psychology of most people.

Our imagination works in two ways: quantitatively or materially when it combines the phantasms of things, and qualitatively when it is concerned with the values and qualities of things. Whereas the first way of using the imagination is that of a workman who is busy with the technical details of his job, the second is evocative and has a power to enchant; it transfigures all things and reveals their secret marvels. Moreover, there is no necessary opposition between these two uses of imagination. In fact, it is quite normal that they be united. The evil in our modern civilization is that the first use is being emphasized at the expense of the second; and the greatest possible harm is that the first use tends to replace the second in the latter's own special domain, that is, in the realm of the arts. This evil is summed up in the word *academicism*. A preoccupation with exact representation, a scientifically detailed attention to perspective and anatomy, is obviously of the quantitative order. It certainly can be a factor in any valid poetic expression, as the past has shown us, but to take this as the criterion, to bend the spirit to its demands as the academicians demand, is the crudest materialism.

A naive idealism has convinced man that he can compensate for his lack of talent by following canons of beauty, rules of composition, conventional systems, and a whole rhetoric of sentiment. All this is of the material order, despite the artist's intentions, because it is mere methodology. His productions ape the current style and are tricked out with a few affectations of originality, because he is reacting according to habit instead of creating anew with each work.

It matters little whether in any one age academicism adopts a narrow, dogmatic system or a broad and seductive eclecticism. It matters little if, having debased all forms of the past, it now embraces "modern" forms of art, leaving behind its fixation for the correct and the finished and fastening on the present taste for what is lazy, muddled, and shapeless. The academicians of 1860 accused the living artists of the time—Delacroix, Corot, Manet—of not finishing their pictures. To this Whistler replied, "Your paintings may be finished, but they are certainly not begun!" The riposte is profoundly true, revealing a distinction between two different orders of things. On the one hand are the academicians, who may undertake enormous pictures which are finished to the last detail, but who are completely unconscious of the real problems involved in their art and completely lacking in any perception of real values. On the other hand, there is precisely the true order of values. And it is important to realize that these values cannot be juxtaposed or superimposed.

Many people think that our schools of art do at least teach the craft of painting, its grammar and syntax, as it were. If the artist who has been through the art school can use all this, as a skillful craftsman uses the instruments of his trade, artists can then express their personal vision. But in fact even this is impossible. Bad habits can become so ingrained that nothing can eradicate them. Art is a mode of being, a qualification of being, for those who are born to create. If the teacher of painting would direct his students to the acquisition and exercise of the material side of art in a way that would help them make their own personal contact with true values, then such teaching would be beneficial. But what most teachers of art do is encourage their young charges to think and act in a manner which is completely false.

Long ago, the Church was fortunate in not having to worry about the quality of art that was used in her service. Until the neo-Classical period, when academicism was beginning to emerge, it was generally true that the best-known artists deserved their renown, and that the finest commissions went to the finest artists. The Church had only to guide the artist to the source of his inspiration and to assist him in being true to it. But in our time the Church, like everyone else, is unworthily served when she approaches those who are *officially* in charge of anything. She has to consider in advance the values of art before commissioning a work. This is evident in the works themselves. For the last century, the more pretentious a work of art for the Church has been, the sooner its poverty has become apparent.

The solution to our problem is not difficult, however. The Church must obviously choose the best, that is, the art which has both vitality and quality. We admit that vitality and quality in art today are rare, but that makes no difference. It simply means that we must be at once more generous and more discerning in our acceptance of art. Our senses, as Matisse has reminded us, are shaped less by our immediate surroundings than by the whole civilization into which we are born. We are endowed with a sensitivity that belongs to this epoch and to no other, and thus our historical period can produce this or that type of work and no other. If we try to perpetuate the forms of the past and insist on speaking a foreign or even a dead language, it means simply that we ourselves are either foreign or dead, as the case may be. But the original artists are always living; their works endure for future generations as a constant source of renewal. It may well be that the forms of the past were technically more beautiful than those of the present, but the pastiches we make today of yesterday's art can never be so great as the truly creative work of the present.

This is the most constant lesson that the history of art teaches. A work of art is timeless only if it truly belongs to its own time. It is a tribute to the greatness of any age (as, for instance, the age of Raphael or Michelangelo) if it can appreciate its own geniuses. Our present age reveals its disharmony precisely in refusing to believe in the art of today as the expression of its true self. Great artists are those who are sensitive to the destiny of the age in which they

live. They are like prophets. If their work survives in the
generations that come after, it means that it has been faithful to the deepest feelings of its own age. But for the last
century, our artists have only scandalized their contemporaries. Even Rembrandt, at first a fashionable painter, was
repudiated by his contemporaries, simply because he allowed his great genius to follow its own course. Who would
dream that the works of Rembrandt that are most ad-
mired today were considered once to be monstrously daring
and offensive? Delacroix's chapel at Saint-Sulpice is youth-
ful and alive and will be as long as it survives, just as it was
in 1861. But even then it caused an outcry. That was because the serious critics of his day were old men, and they
promised eternity only to those who could remind them of
the past. The walls of many a nineteenth-century church
still offer us pathetic echoes of what in Florence, Venice,
and Rome was living beauty.

We should not, of course, take the view opposed to that
of our scandalized contemporaries just for its own sake. The
avant-garde is not necessarily good art. We must accommodate our whole being in a positive manner to the works
in which genius expresses itself and to the values which are
involved. Often we find, even among cultivated people, that
the importance of accommodation to works of art is not at
all appreciated. The eye always needs to get used to a new
distance or a new gradation of light. This cannot be called a
subjective approach if we consider that it is the conditions
of objects that determine the mechanism of our faculties of
knowledge. After we have been deeply moved, let us say, by

a work of Victor Hugo, the qualities of Racine will force us to make some adjustment.

For the last century, the public has refused to accommodate itself. Many people have insisted to me that the values of art are immediately perceived! They agreed that works of art should be allowed to grow on us, but insisted nevertheless that the immediate impact conveys everything essential. And they have maintained that if something which at first appeared shocking grows on us in the course of time, the initial shock remains a valid reaction, since one can get used to anything. But this is just another way of refusing to accept the new—a refusal which contradicts our dignity as human beings. For we are called upon to enliven our minds, our feelings, and our hearts, to maintain an awareness which will not allow habit to be reduced to mere mechanical responses. Man is not asked to abdicate his judgment on the value of works of art or to accept everything uncritically, but rather to be so awakened to what is new, so alive to quality, that the mind will be freed both from its servitude to opinions inherited from the undiscriminating crowd and from the influence of fads.

But whether we accommodate ourselves or not, either the values of art are new or they are not values at all. We may dream our Gothic dreams, we may be attached as ever to our favorite pictures "that help us pray best" and to our sumptuous church interiors; nevertheless, we must try to see what the artists of today are giving us that is valuable. We must be grateful for the best that they give us, even while we remind them constantly of the demands of the faithful, of sacred art, of the highest sources of inspiration, and of the liturgy.

The facts of any era of art can no more be rejected than can the climate. For the last hundred years, people have been trying to ignore these facts, to minimize their importance or to compromise them. This has had the effect, in Guzzi's words, of producing in the church an art that is marginal and anachronistic; but even worse, it has given rise to the "renaissance of sacred art" which we find in all its discord in our churches and in one exhibition after another. On the other hand, every time we become ready to accept the fact that we are living in an era of poverty, such glorious things as Odilon Redon's "Sacred Heart," the works of Rouault and Denis, and the Chapel of the Holy Angels present themselves. These are the great examples, and there are many lesser names that could be mentioned. One must, as Delacroix reminds us, accept the possibility of genius. Genius is capable of expressing itself in different degrees and different styles. Whenever these geniuses of our time have been called upon to work for the Church, the result has had universal appeal and value in the measure of its uniqueness and permanence even though it has been condemned for its daring newness.

In short, we should do exactly the opposite of what we habitually do. Instead of devising some ideal of the Church completely divorced from time, an ideal based on abstract theological principles or, more often, alas, on obsolete historical conditions, let us simply see what our creators can give us that is genuine. Let us embrace the principle that our recent popes have adopted for indigenous art in mission countries; native art has been welcomed as long as it was not contrary to the faith.[3] Obviously, whatever they may be worth in themselves, living works of art reflecting their own time are far more valuable to men than any reminiscences of the past, even though the past may have been in every way better than the present. The dog was the most contemptible of beasts to the Jews; yet they had the proverb, "A living dog is better than a dead lion".[4]

[3] See "Le douloureux Problème des Arts missionnaires," L'Art Sacré, March, 1951.

[4] Eccles. 9:4.

8

ART AS A FREE LANGUAGE

An essential and ancient concept of art was that it is a way of making something according to a certain method or certain procedures; and there are correct ways, *certae viae*, which are predetermined and fixed. From this it followed that if one knew the ways, one *possessed* one's art, like a material good or a skill; one practiced the "rules of art." Thus, the "arts" were quite easily paired with the "crafts." It was not until the Renaissance that the "fine arts" were set aside for the disinterested pursuit of "beauty;" but when this was done, the beauty the artist felt dedicated to achieve was an approved beauty, which again demanded its own rules and procedures, so that the fine arts entailed just as prescribed a technique as the arts and crafts before them.

By the nineteenth century, however, the masters had come to realize quite clearly that the value of a work of art in any age lies in its expression of qualities which no one can determine, let alone classify. There is an imponderable something that has nothing at all to do with rules. There is beauty, without any doubt whatever, but not a prescribed beauty. And the effect that the nineteenth-century painters

prized in the works of their age was something purified from
all the conventions which in the past had tended to become
a substitute for great art.

The beauty of Cézanne's "Card Players," for instance,
obviously does not lie in the models he used or their poses;
neither is it in the virtuosity with which he copied his
models, or in any nobility of style, or in his particularly ingenious use of color. The beauty of this picture lies simply
in the fact that there is a harmony in the painting which
has value in itself. Every element is transfigured in the
harmony at which the painter aimed. And the painter's
mind and heart are apparent in all the elements as we examine them in turn. Every stroke of the brush has Cézanne's whole personality behind it; it was, one feels, exactly
that stroke and no other that the picture demanded. One
is conscious of a deliberate refusal to let convention dictate
anything, because the dictates of convention could in no
way help. But for anyone looking at the picture with eyes
and mind conditioned by the accepted canons of taste in
Cézanne's day, there was probably no proportion, no integrity, no splendor. For anyone who looks at it without the
approved canons at the back of his mind, these three traditional characteristics of the beautiful are there with the full-
est possible force.

Art, at this level, is more than ever *technique*, but the
whole of the technique is at the service of that ineffable
quality rather than any particular artistic convention. Every
accepted formula must be rejected, since each work—indeed, each fresh stroke of the brush as the artist produces
it—is something fresh and new; in other words, an inven-

tion. Rouault's definition of a craft is "the accord between the perceptible world and a certain inner illumination." It is not a conglomeration of undifferentiated procedures which might be applicable to all works of art. Nonetheless, we can say that art today is more than ever technique. It is identified with technique and it will not accept the academic distinction between form and content. The form is the content.[1] Anecdote and sentiment are not part of it. Art is simply the achievement of a work. But every stroke of the brush is created by a living mind, aware of its own mystery and tending toward the mystery of things and the mystery of the work which is being produced here and now. The artist looks for his "inner illumination" in and through the perceptible.[2]

During the nineteenth-century development of art, Europe was introduced to a great variety of hitherto unfamiliar forms from Asia and Africa and from primitive and tribal cultures. And it became quite evident at last that the esthetic of the Renaissance (which was bound, sooner or later, to decline into a purely academic mold) had been all the time like a spotlight, illuminating exclusively one small family of works of art and leaving the rest of our artistic heritage in complete darkness. Art in our time has made contact with forms which express a more primitive and more direct mode of being. These forms are the very

[1] Henri Focillon, *Piero della Francesca*, p. 57.
[2] Père Couturier, writing in *L'Art Sacré* (July, 1951, p. 26), tells how Matisse discovered that painting could be a language, and aspire to be nothing more than that if need be, while he was looking at the Goyas in the Musée de Lille.

negation of all our academic conventions inherited from the Renaissance. The disproportionate figures that are, academically speaking, clumsy and ugly are of the essence of these forms, and are necessary for the works in question. The mode of being involved in these works requires a disregard for perspective and an absolute simplicity, and nothing else could take their place.

Although contemporary artists have revolted against the Renaissance mode of being, the viewing public is even worse than Renaissance in its outlook, since it has become conditioned by that degenerate academicism which characterized the Renaissance at its worst. This being the case, some people argue that the artist must meet the demands of the public halfway, using, as it were, a minimum of contemporary artistic grammar and syntax to make himself understood. But however desirable this might be, the opportunities are becoming less and less frequent, simply because this particular period is, in Matisse's phrase, the age of the development of the senses. It is not an age concerned with the "proper" things; it is in reality a "primitive" period. The artist cannot escape this fact, because he feels the spirit of the age more strongly than anyone else.

The evolution of art for the last century has been away from the conventional treatment of forms. There is a reaction against the objective world, particularly since in our time the world tends to enslave men. In this highly mechanized age, the artist, who reacts more strongly than the mass of men, is bound to demonstrate his own individuality and nature. His contacts are always immediate, his reactions strong and vivid.

A feeling for the sacred also militates against the spirit of the Renaissance and helps liberate the plastic language the artist uses. Obviously, when the Renaissance spirit was alive and valid, the transcendent character of the sacred could use it easily enough. On the contrary, academicism and the genuine expression of the sacred are absolutely incompatible, as we see most clearly in the many unfortunate instances of virtuosity for its own sake and the artist's slavery to a conventional ideal of beauty. This virtuosity, this "slick vulgarity,"[3] this proud excess of materialism is the logical outcome of academicism. Fashionable prettiness cannot represent anything spiritual. It proceeds from vanity, and can only produce more vanity. St. John of the Cross castigates the mentality which becomes enamored of some pretty rosary only to discard it when something prettier is offered.[4] This is far removed from the Gospel—as far removed, indeed, as virtuosity is from art.

The pseudo-Platonic myth of beauty is perhaps even more dangerous than academicism and virtuosity because it seems a trifle more "spiritual." It is certainly the cause of many dangerous and foolish misunderstandings in art. The Renaissance spirit pays homage to beauty as if it were a divine attribute, but in fact beauty is only divine if we can prevent ourselves from treating it as an idol and from giving it divine honors. And beauty becomes an idol as soon as we imagine that there is a type of beauty, elaborated by the mind of man, which must be present in every variation

[3] Joseph Samson, *Musique et Vie intérieure* (Paris: La Colombe, 1951), p. 221.
[4] *The Ascent of Mt. Carmel*, bk. III, pt. 2, chap. 34.

which we make on the beautiful. As soon as we set out to make beauty the end and purpose of our works of art instead of hoping humbly that it will occur in the work of art as a gratuitous overflow, it is no longer a divine attribute but a purely profane object, the result of unaided human industry. Conventional and laboriously achieved, such beauty takes us no further than itself, whereas true beauty, the humble beauty that comes as an unexpected, unmerited gift, is a means to something beyond itself. It can occur only when the artist is open to the infinite in the act of his creation. His openness must be so real that of itself it will necessarily break down every established academic convention. It cannot depend on industry alone, but on something that is very near to grace and is certainly a free gift.

Estheticism is a false attitude, and it would be sacrilegious if it were not so naive. It is lamentable to see a church full of supposedly "fine art," put there because some priest has said to himself, "Beauty is the splendor of the true" and "Art imitates nature." Why can people not see that art imitates not nature as such but nature's mode of working, transposing this mode to its own sphere?[5] The academic vision of beauty is so limited, so pathetically dependent on appearance, that it prevents any contact with the sacred.

In general terms, the incompatibility of academicism and the sacred is of two sorts. Either the artist copies nature servilely, or he tries to embellish nature. Thus, there is always a compromise between false transcendence and a re-

[5] One can use a scholastic distinction and say that art imitates not *natura naturata* but *natura naturans*.

fusal to admit transcendence. In contrast to academicism, there is a very close affinity between the art of today and the spirit of Christianity, and therefore a great aptitude for such art to open itself to the sacred. As Régine Pernoud writes:

Today, we know that the secret is not in an exact copy or in any illusory embellishment but in transfiguration. Painting . . . transmutes the elements of the world, not by taking them back to their prototype but on the contrary by giving them their true individuality. . . . In our world, in which each individual tends to be dissolved into anonymity and the abstract and the collective are constantly emphasizing uniformity, painting proclaims . . . that everything is *exceptional*, and that there is not a single face, not a ray of light, no familiar object which cannot become, by the painter's art, a dazzling piece of individuality. . . .

Van Gogh's kitchen chair and Picasso's handlebars seem to transcend the everyday world of which they were once part. The painter saw them, and that was enough to make them what they are now. Painters of the past would look for so-called noble and elevating subjects, but a painter can confer nobility on everything he touches. Painting, seen in this light, is analogous to holiness, which in turn can never be conceived as conformity to an ideal type but must always be seen as the transfiguration of the whole personality, in which the individual becomes more fully what he is under the influence of grace.

The magic of painting is that it does not draw its strength from external elements, which are only means to its end, but from an effort of the inner man—"from what he has got inside him," as Matisse says. The same painters who have helped us rediscover nature teach us that we become creators not by looking about us, seeking out models, but by looking within ourselves so as to find there the great unwritten laws. . . . Contemporary art is born of the interior life. Whatever the painter puts on his canvas, be it a bunch of vegetables or a guitar, it is always the fruit of his inner experience, and this can never be replaced by

any canon or rule of art. Painting today begins at the point
where every artist sets out to be the first man to put paint to
canvas. He has to find in himself, and by himself, the gift of
creation that is deposited in man, created as he is in the image of
God."[6]

There are two additional features of the greatest importance to be observed. First of all, the primary aim of plastic
art today is the reproduction not of appearances but of a
truth which surpasses the truths apparent to our senses.
Perspective, for instance, was used for putting things in the
place where the eye situated them, just as a camera situates
things with its lens. But the compositions of today, like
those of the pre-Classical era, are governed by the mind and
the spirit of man, not by his eye alone. With this primacy of
spiritual over material observation, the antinomy between
the knowing subject and the object of knowledge tends
to disappear. The painter becomes one with his creation.
Instead of seeking contour and tactile values, he follows out
a rhythm. Matisse, let us say, sees an oak leaf, and he draws
it. At first the drawing is an exact copy of the leaf; then, as
he goes on repeating the sketch, the modulations of the leaf
come by instinct, and these modulations are to the leaf
what the soul is to the body, both its form and its essence.
It is a rhythm that now lives in the artist and belongs to
him. And it flows from the artist of itself, from within like a
prayer. There was a time when all art was prayer, but that
was in the days before Classicism.

This helps us realize how deeply and intensely modern

[6] Régine Pernoud, in *L'Art Sacré*, January, 1950, p. 14.

art may become an act of worship. The following chapters will confirm this view, but before going further it would be perhaps advisable to consider some objections.

The task of the arts today is so fundamentally serious that this in itself should warn us to expect but few successful achievements. Few artists are capable of withstanding the rigors, demands, and frustrations that art imposes upon them. There are many failures, and many works baffle us because we cannot see what they mean. I do not mean that we cannot see what they represent; I mean that the special characteristics of the intuition from which these works proceed demand an accommodation that takes more time than we have at our disposal.

One is tempted to add that every artist is forced to be either a creator or nothing at all. But creative geniuses are rare in every age. In times past, second- and third-rate artists could still produce work according to their modest means for many useful purposes. They were commissioned to do work that was not beyond their powers, and they did it well. But today all the influences in the world of art tend to demand an originality of artists which very few really possess. This, however, is not the fault of contemporary art but of the artists concerned. The only two forms of art apparent today are living art and dead academicism. Outside the ranks of truly talented artists, it is impossible to find a minor artist modestly producing modest work that is really worthwhile. The only artists worthy of note are the experimentalists, who go their own dangerous way. Among them we find every tendency and all grades of talent. Artistic talent and inventive gifts are dangerous things now-adays. Outside this battleground, there is nothing.

But despite all the failures and the uncertainties, there has been undeniable progress since the nineteenth century and the beginning of the twentieth. We have only to look at what that period has furnished for our museums and churches. Progress has in fact been enormous since, under men like Maurice Denis, it has been a progress from nothing. If the artist refuses to take the risks of hazardous creation, he can only give us a "modernistic" rendering of the empty forms of the past which will be either insignificant or aggressive.

Risks must be taken, and they are great, but there is hope nevertheless. The basic difficulties can be turned to great advantage in some cases. However, there is one problem that reveals a fundamental divergence between contemporary art and certain tasks which the Church requires of artists. The plastic forms now enjoying such great freedom are pure creative gestures expressing their own mysterious individuality. They can certainly reveal the mystery of things, but at the same time they are not concerned with appearances. But most people need appearances if they are to be at all interested in things. Above all, popular piety can only accept representations of the familiar. A working parish has a right to its statue of St. Joseph, as I have said. Whom shall we commission to do it? There is no doubt that some special spiritual feature of St. Joseph would be admirably revealed in a work by Henri Laurens or Germaine Richier, and it would be so sincere and true that many of the people in that parish would love it when they had become accustomed to it. But many more would never get over their initial shock. Simplicity in the beholder is all too often covered with a thick layer of conditioning by long habits that took root even before childhood.

But the problem can be graver still. The reason the faithful want representational art is not primarily because we have been conditioned by an academic background but because we live in the sphere of the Word made flesh. The normal, simple Christian soul expects works of art to provide images of the invisible truths of the faith by which we live. If the plastic arts cannot give us representation, we cannot expect anything else to provide our imaginations with the forms of our daily life, transfigured by the visitation of God into this world of the flesh. Unfortunately, the plastic arts do not fulfill this mission today; but there is nothing that can be done about it, simply because the art of today is looking in other directions. Art evolves in a seasonal cycle, and the present phase is a nonrepresentational one.

If we look for works of art produced in our time that are on a technical level with the works of the past, copying the forms of nature and attempting a close likeness of human expression, we must admit that all they attain is sterility, sentimentality, or grimace. The care with which artists of the past sought to express some feeling seems in no way to have interfered with their technical result. But if one claims now to have anything like the figures that enchant one in Gothic sculpture, all one has in fact is crude expressionism or whimsicality. And this is because art today is following quite another path. It is as if the past excesses of pseudo-idealism and naturalism demanded expiation in our own time, a reaction that will do penance for a too facile spirituality with its sentimental illusions. And because of this, even the legitimate Christian feeling for the sphere of the Incarnation in which we have our being is frustrated. The only choice today seems to be between unworthy expressions of this Incarnation and an art so purified that nothing in the ordinary life of the pious man prepares him to appreciate it. That is why so many Christians do not know where they are in the matter of art and suppose that all artists have gone mad. But they always have their standby in the cheap, pretentious repository art.

The needs which art cannot now ordinarily satisfy are admittedly accidental needs, but we must realize what *accidental* means here. The word is not to be used lightly, for accidental qualities are for most Christians the most normal means of finding their way to the essential, at least insofar as art plays any part at all in their lives. This part, as I have already said, is to dispose Christians to celebrate in the most effective and fruitful way the mystery in which they are made one with Christ. In this, the arts speak to their feelings so as to bring them into play. Emotions can easily militate against the spirit, but they can, thanks to the arts, be a help to the spirit too. Needless to say, living art acts both directly on our senses and also at a deeper level. Now, if art claims to transport the faithful to God without intermediary images like Bethlehem and Calvary, such art might just as well not exist as far as most Christians are concerned. This is not a tragedy, since the plastic arts do not play a decisive role in life. I have already said that the functions of these arts have been replaced by other and more compelling media. Experience has proved that men of this industrial age have rediscovered in themselves the fundamental love of rhythm, significant gesture, and attitudes in which the spiritual and the perceptible interpenetrate, and when contemplating really good works of art in the non-objective manner of today they find an affinity with these works at a much deeper level than that of their everyday piety. Thus, art calls with a prophetic voice, appealing to us to enter into our own souls. But few there are who listen.

9

The Artist's Inner Voice

"An artist," as Rouault expressed it, "must obey his inner voice." This is the most fundamental need of the artist of today. We can profitably read again the words which Rilke wrote in the first of his "Letters to a Young Poet":

A work of art is good if it has sprung from necessity. In this nature of its origin lies its judgment; there is no other. Therefore, . . . go into yourself and test the deeps in which your life takes rise; at its source you will find the answer to the question of whether you must create. Accept it, just as it sounds, without trying to interpret it. Perhaps it will turn out that you are called to be an artist. Then take that destiny upon yourself and bear it, its burden and its greatness, without ever asking what recompense might come from outside. For the creator must be a world for himself and find everything in himself and in nature with whom he has allied himself. . . .

What more shall I say to you? Everything seems to me to have its just emphasis; and after all, I do only want to advise you to keep growing quietly and seriously throughout your development; you cannot disturb it more rudely than by looking outward and expecting from outside replies to questions that only your inmost feeling in your quietest hours can perhaps answer.[1]

[1] Rainer Maria Rilke, letter dated Paris, February 17, 1903, in *Letters to a Young Poet*, tr. M. D. Herter Norton (New York: Norton, 1934), pp. 18–19.

The true artist expresses only what he feels, and feels in the moment of expression. To quote Rouault again, he spends "his life trying to find the true and appropriate means of expressing *his* gifts and *his* temperament."[2]

Nothing of any value in art can be drawn from any other place than these depths of the self. One could wish that contemporary art might offer some easier way, but in fact only the "inner voice" can inspire a real artist's creation, in our time as in any other. If we should presume to tell the artist to obey some other voice, he would have nothing to say. And the obligation to obey the inner voice is more imperative in religious art than in any other. Artistic creation is like mystical experience. The artist is led "where he would prefer not to go," and gropes "in a dark and silent night." Even Nicholas Poussin, the most lucidly self-willed of painters, wrote, "No one can gather the golden bough unless he is led to it by Fate."[3] The work of art is something not only willed but suffered, undergone. The artist's will finds its highest freedom in submitting to this obedience. The artist is the first to be amazed by what springs from the depths of his being. How much more is it bound to amaze the viewer when the "inner voice" compels the artist, as it may well do, to defy convention and to transcend appearance? But the artist has no alternative.

[2] Written in 1937, and quoted in *La Renaissance* magazine.
[3] This is Virgil's golden bough, which no one can pluck who is not led to it by Fate. Poussin speaks of the parts of painting which cannot be learned, and which are the most precious things in the painter's art. Among these he includes not only grace but even likeness and judgment, which one would suppose can be acquired by dint of application. The whole text of Poussin is given in Pierre du Colombier's *Les plus beaux Écrits des grands Artistes* (1946), p. 12.

Such is the resemblance between artistic creation and mystical experience that one may well be unable to decide which of the following notions is more correct. (1) Any art that obeys the inner voice is necessarily fated to move toward what is genuinely sacred. In the act of translating the Christian mystery, the artist will find his own fulfillment, and we will behold a renewal of Christian art of unprecedented depth and power. (2) The resemblance between artistic and mystical experience can be a false one, a mere trick, and art, once it has taken this direction, can only become Christian by a total conversion and by humility to a degree that may subvert the work of art.

Whichever notion is the more valid, one thing is sure: the artist can only find his way to the sacred by way of the paths I have described. In any work of art, the sacred character consists in the quality of the forms produced. This quality comes directly from the dispositions of the artist's mind and heart—which is to say, art is a mode of being. I do not mean simply the good moral dispositions that influence the artist as a man. Quite often a "Christian artist" in people's minds is just an artist who chooses pious subjects. But this is not enough. The sacred quality of a work of art must come out in the very forms the artist uses, quite independently of his themes. These forms and their quality are the result of the artist's obedience to his inner voice. They are what he undergoes almost more than what he produces. He is the victim of some transcendent force which commands him to leave his country and the place of his people.[4] For this reason, the artist can only expect the

4 Gen. 12:1.

sacred character of his work to come from his fidelity to the inner voice, to the impulse from the depths of his soul.

Many people, unfortunately, have the prejudice that the creative experience is a monstrous presumption, an arrogant claim to powers that do not belong to man the creature but only to the divine Creator. There seems to be something Promethean about the artist's obeying his inner voice. On the subject of the new churches at Assy and Vence, Marcel de Corte wrote,

> Modern man has broken the age-old alliance that bound his being to the real world and its Creator. He is making another world for himself, which he is drawing out of his own substance. The more he loses his living contact with the reality about him, the more he projects his overworked, self-centered imagination into politics and art. . . .
> For many Christians, everything that distorts nature in society, politics, or art is an initiation into the divine, and everything that is contrary to nature leads to the supernatural. The religion of the Incarnation is gradually turning into a religion of disincarnation.[5]

Against this we can argue that nothing authorizes us to suppose that the artist is presuming to use his liberty beyond the limits of his creaturehood. His "autonomy" can in fact be very humble and open to the world. We can also argue that it is wrong to speak of "modern art" or "modern artists" en bloc. The Promethean mystique which well-meaning people reproach our artists for is certainly not

[5] Marcel de Corte, in Libre Belgique, February 5, 1952.

professed by people like Matisse, Rouault, Bazaine, and Manessier.

Usually, we can lay the ghost of Prometheus wherever the critics find him, and he is no more than a ghost. But we must admit that the fear of a too strongly marked individuality is a real one. But individualism there must be, and the fact that it can be a danger in no way militates against its very real promises and possibilities.

The necessity of individualism comes from the fact that in a materialistic, totalitarian, and mechanized world, man must look for his salvation in works that offer him the opportunity of finding new and deeper dimensions in himself. As long as the spirit of man is not completely stifled, art will tend more and more to take this direction, and this tendency will always seem to be something of a revolt— which it is, of course, but only in the way that the Gospel is a revolt. It is a necessary revolt, and like the Gospel it deepens the inner world of mankind in a way that is personal to each individual. In individualism, art is granted its full liberty to create, and today, "Art can be nothing but individualistic, given the demands of our time."[6]

As far as religious art is concerned, the dangers of too strong an individuality need not be emphasized. The chief risk is that artists may cut themselves off from tradition and lose themselves outside the boundaries of faith in their own fancies. That this has happened proves that the danger exists. The odd thing is that some Catholics justify such a departure in theory. Their aim, they claim, is to bring back

[6] Alfred Manessier, *L'Art religieux actual* (booklet, Servir series; Toulouse, 1948), p. 7.

into the Church the overflowing and abundant life of modern art. But it is still necessary to demand that art in the Church be specifically Christian. Some have supposed that the inner voice and the truths of faith must necessarily be of two different realms, that faith involves a specialized world where inspiration may get lost. This is the sort of contradiction with which Modernism can corrupt religious art. Its ultimate expression, calmly accepted by some, is that henceforth in the Church there must exist side by side an empty orthodoxy and an art whose very life depends on neglecting orthodoxy. On the one hand would be liturgy and preaching as clerical prerogatives, with a debased art completely subservient to the rules of faith; on the other, an art whose mission was to bring to the Church some reflection of the perceptiveness and the living religious current of the layman's world. This art is meant to be accepted in the Church, even though it is "not exactly Christian." The solution of this problem cannot be in any compromise of principle. Only by deepening and broadening our outlook can we find the way out.

Some complain against our individualists of today that the artists of the past did all they could to resemble their predecessors, and this being the case, they could put their works in a church in the full knowledge that continuity was being maintained. Contemporary artists, it is said, seem to want only to resemble themselves, and so they cut themselves off from the one thing that can guarantee the sacred character of a work—tradition. This is a typical instance of muddled thinking. A superficial glance sees nothing but a violent break between Courbet and Monet and Monet and

Cézanne, and still greater breaks later, while it finds a strong family resemblance among all pieces of "museum art." But the desire to imitate one's predecessors is only a foolish myth, as foolish as the idea that contemporary painters want, on principle, to be different from their forebears. In either case, it is a question of the artist's being faithful to his vocation, which is unique to himself alone. If artists in times past tended to produce their works in a more or less common mold, this was because they shared a way of life and an outlook which was taken as much for granted as the climate and the place in which they lived. On the other hand, of course, a sense of continuity can be very desirable and may even help the individualist in art from becoming pretentiously mediocre. Some, but not all, have been fortunate enough to find the means for true expression and for everything necessary to their temperament and their gifts. And of course the fact that we have no traditional corpus of artistic procedure does not bar a certain spirit of tradition in art.

An important incidental fact to which this leads us is that collaboration has become difficult, although everything depends on the individualism in question and the purpose for which collaboration is envisaged. Where we find discord among the juxtaposed elements of a church decor which has been realized by several hands, it means quite often that the artists in question have not yet reached agreement in themselves. Thus far, the groups of artists who have banded together into a sort of parody of the craft guilds of the Middle Ages have tended to spoil themselves by a priori theorizing. And when a genius finds it impossible to work with a group, there is nothing new in that. The actual conditions of the work to be done may make collaboration impossible, or it may be the imponderables of creation itself. The artist, as an individual, is still groping in his own obscure world, so it is hard on him to be expected to collaborate with others at this stage. His individualism is, likely as not, simply part of the mystic quality of his creation, and not at all due to a simple determination to be original and different.

We see two conceptions of ecclesiastical art arising that are fundamentally opposed to each other. Once they were reconcilable, but not today. One conception considers the work at hand in its material aspect; thus, an artist is commissioned to produce forty stained-glass windows or the mosaics for a whole basilica. According to the other conception, the artist lives in the depths in which his work takes shape, following the hard demands of his inner vision. No collaborator or helper could share in such a work. The material conditions of life today, as well as artistic factors, all help to cheapen the first kind of mass enterprise, even if the artist's intention is pure. As for the creative genius, the more seriously he takes his work, the more humbly he limits himself and communes with his soul in silence.

How then are we to make the most of this modern individualism? Are we to oblige Rouault to make us a "beautiful" Christ on the pretext that the faithful must have it so? When our Rouaults are accused of individualism, it

usually means that many Christians are very strongly and
humanly obsessed by the security they find in certain forms
they are accustomed to.

This is a single instance of the conflict between the individual and the Church, a conflict which can only continue when the individual walls himself up in his self-
sufficiency and the Church makes itself known only by its
outer appearance. But the deep personality opening itself
up to the realities by which the Church lives finds in them
its most individual fulfillment. The inner life of a man is
perfected by communion with God and with other men.

It is important to remember that the artist's obedience to
the inner voice need not make him act like a little tin
god. A man's freedom is still the freedom of a creature conditioned by factors other than himself. The inner voice is
much more likely to call the artist to welcome influences
from without, to mistrust himself, than to puff him up with
pride. Many artists find that the inner voice is more or less
explicitly a Christian inspiration. When they are offered
a sacred theme, they take to it immediately. They choose
such themes willingly, and show by the way they treat
them that they really do understand them. And for a
painter like Rouault, a Catholic by birth and conviction,
the inner voice compelled him to feel and to be in fact
a true child of the Church. If you lead an artist from outside the Church to her liturgy, to her great teaching, to the
message of her saints throughout the ages and the communion of her people, he will find in these the very well-
spring of his own renewal and nothing to frustrate him. He

will feel a new life coming into him, and will at last be sincerely, wholeheartedly caught up in a new orientation to the supernatural.

"Love and do what you will" is basically a principle for individualists. The more one takes this principle seriously, the more it appears orthodox, or at least capable of becoming orthodox. Since an artist's vocation is a call to the work which must be produced, we have reasonable grounds for optimism about the adoption of the principle. An artist only asks to assimilate the data which governs his creation. As Valéry said, he would be a poor artist if he were not the plaything of his own work.[7] He identifies himself with the sacred, and as Matisse remarked, he should be so familiar with things like the stations of the cross as to be able to paint them blindfolded.[8] In 1948, and this is even more interesting, Matisse said to Frère Rayssiguier, "God is holding my hand, so I am not responsible for my work." The brother answered, "In that case, why do you not try painting a religious subject, the Virgin, for instance? You would be certain to produce something good because, as you say, God is holding your hand." But this the painter denied. "I don't feel such subjects yet. If I painted them, it would be myself laying down what I did. My own will would be too involved in it. When I paint a profane subject, God is certainly leading me and so I can get beyond myself. But if I were to paint the Blessed Virgin, it would be because I was forcing myself to do so, and God would leave me to my own devices." Only three months after, Matisse felt obliged

[7] Paul Valéry, in Variété, V, 121.
[8] Henri Matisse, in L'Art Sacré, July, 1951, p. 16.

to design a whole chapel. Starting with the idea of a design for the windows, he was to work out over the course of more than three years the plans for decorating the whole building.

As this case shows us, the artist must imbibe the sources of his work from the beginning of his remote preparation.[9] All too often, when an artist is commissioned to do a religious work, he complains that the priests in charge do not give a sufficiently clear idea of what they want, while later on they spare no criticism of the fact that the artist has too pronounced a bias in a certain direction. Those who commissioned it would have prevented this misunderstanding if their instructions had been more explicit at the outset. A good artist always prefers a thoroughly clear-cut idea of what is wanted. Nor do artists, as we tend to fear, show any sign of being put off by the rigorous demands of liturgical legislation.

Indeed, individualism does much more good than harm in sacred art if it is deep enough to merit the title *personalism*. In its depths, it is open to the supernatural. This is the artistic equivalent of the general law that only the *person* is capable of this receptivity, even though *person* is defined by the very features that make it a closed entity. The "personal" artist is aware of the value in the themes he is asked to depict and of the functions involved in the Church's worship. He sees these things in their deepest necessity, and far from being obsessed by his own singularity, he becomes most scrupulous in his efforts to satisfy in every way the demands which the Church, both clergy and faithful, make

[9] See Chapter 13 of the present work for Bonnard's experience painting St. Francis de Sales.

of him. He cares about such things in a way that is startlingly deep and genuine and touching. But he can only do so if he is utterly committed to his inner voice, to his need to create.

As I said before, inner necessity leads the artist along ways that are unfamiliar. He is not at all sure of the direction in which he is going. At first sight this seems to be a far cry from the assurance an artist would have had in times past, following the *certae viae*. But there is not such a great difference, in fact, between these two situations; nothing essential is affected. There is only a change of emphasis from making to creating: whereas a work used to be *made*, now it would rather appear to be *born*, at least insofar as the true artist is concerned. This is the difference between academic art on the one hand and, on the other, classic and primitive art. Academic art is *made*, and even though to all intents and purposes classic or primitive art may appear to the artist as process of making rather than creating, its genesis is in fact as mysterious as the birth of any living thing.

The words of Jean Bazaine on this subject in his *Notes sur la Peinture d'Aujourd'hui* express my point:

Although discovery may often be a matter of chance, there is no room for chance in the process of artistic invention. Everything that happens in that process is prompted by the urge to follow a strictly necessary order. We may have only the obscurest intuition of what we are about, but this very intuition involves us in an inevitable series of steps which we must follow through a darkness in which our intelligence can give us no help at all. We are thus led within ourselves to what is most personal to us and at the same time most universal in us. We have the impression of recognizing the pictures we paint little by little, and we never know in advance what exactly will be the outcome of our efforts. . . .

All painters, whether representational or not, provided they conceive of painting as a sort of incarnation, are familiar with this slow groping. . . . A body lying in the grass may become a tree against the sky, . . . and suddenly there is life in a subject which, until that moment, had no life. . . .

How many painters, and some of them the greatest, simply allow themselves to be led in the darkness, drawn by some intense but unformulated sensation that begins with one or two undisciplined strokes of the brush. The finished work was no doubt somehow present in the unconscious mind, and although the conscious mind has the mastery of it, it could not have given birth to the work, nor could it foretell exactly what shape it would take. . . .

Art is first formulated in the unconscious, before the artist realizes any clear form in his mind. Some painters are conscious of each new step in the work being taken under the compulsion of a power over which they have no command. . . . For the artist, sincerity means letting himself be led in this way, without knowing whither. But sincerity also implies facing up to his own limitations, which will be the limitations of his era as well. A genius will not run away from limitations, but will do all he can to reach out to them, and go beyond them if he can. . . .

Each phase in the history of painting has its own limitations. These are its special domain, and constitute the task it is given to accomplish. The only times that Delacroix painted badly were when he thought himself a contemporary of Titian. Cézanne is a superb example of the painter who is constantly throwing himself against what he believes are his limitations in an effort to burst through them. We must not try to be primitive unless we are certain that we deserve to be. And we can leave the "committed" painters to their pointless service of ideals irrelevant to art.

An artist does not produce the work he wishes to produce. He desires intensely to produce the maximum that art can produce in his era. And this can only happen through the obscure striving of instinct and feelings. It has nothing to do with knowledge or familiarity with art history. One rule alone is supreme: each new picture must be a start from the very beginning. It certainly makes a difficult world in which to work, full of demands and lacking in light, and it is no wonder that every age of art tries to avoid it, to find facile solutions. . . .[10]

One of the most welcome points to emerge from Bazaine's remarks is that the old Platonist concept of the work of art existing in the artist's mind as something conscious, distinct, entirely willed by the artist, and then translated into matter is shown to be too naive to have any value for us. The analogy between artistic creation and birth is particularly valid in that human initiative can make the best use possible of the means at our disposal, but we never know what sort of child will result. The role of the conscious mind in this creation can be enormous; this "control" which Bazaine speaks of will vary according to the temperament of the artist, and it will always be steeped in the perceptible world. Another very interesting point is the artist's progressive recognition of his work as he creates it. Perhaps most remarkable of all is the fact that Bazaine seems to combine personal creation with the life of art in a given period and the acceptance of limitations with invention. Here are four obviously distinct qualities, but they are certainly a unity in the artist's experience.

We can draw two major conclusions at this point. First, it is apparent that we cannot believe in the possibility of an art commited to any particular manifesto, social, political,

[10] Jean Bazaine, *Notes sur la Peinture d'Aujourd'hui* (Paris: Fleury, 1948), pp. 25–26, 34–35.

or otherwise. This is the point we shall take up next. Second, it is difficult to apply art to predetermined tasks. This is obvious if we hold the view that the outcome is always impossible to foretell, that success is uncertain. This has always been the case, but it was never more imperative than today. Unfortunately, the supposition that an artist will provide anything to order, as if he were a tradesman, is as current as it ever was.

Sacred art is already doubly committed. It is first of all essentially tied to its thematic material and determined by it. Second, it is in the service of a determined cause. Moreover, it must be very conscious of being involved in this double program—conscious, that is, of its function and of the objects it uses. Dogma directs its every movement, and the service it renders makes it necessarily a sincere language of faith and piety. The human causes for which men sacrifice themselves today are fanatically totalitarian, and consequently it is taken for granted that they have the right to debase art on the pretext that artists must be committed to political movements and social programs. The debased art that the "committed" artist produces comes as the result of a conflict between his political or social convictions and the inner voice which must always command his creation.

There is no reason, of course, that the inner necessity which drives him on should not be in some way qualified by his convictions. All we ask is that the artist's work not suffer from his political and social ideas, and that these not exercise constraint, or act as a sidetrack, or weaken his art or change it for the worse. Courbet's revolutionary convictions are always quite obvious in such works as "The Stone-breakers," "The Workshop," and "The Burial at Ornans," but as a painter he managed to keep his freedom. Such an achievement is unusual. More often we find that the artist's alliance with ideas—and particularly ideas irrelevant to art—leads him to an abstracting outlook at the expense of perceptible qualities. Sentimentality enters his work, and propagandist passions and other extraneous motives corrupt his inner judgment just as they vitiate the judgment of the partisans for whose benefit the work was produced. Artistic imposture is always likely to take the place of sincerity when the artist's conviction transcends the realities of his imagination and of his sensitivities. Nazi art, the Socialist realism of the U.S.S.R., and the art that we normally find in churches are the three most dreadful manifestations of art that our century has witnessed. To be subjected to the tastes of the masses or the control of political absolutism constitutes the worst possible living conditions for an artist.

We have to ask ourselves seriously if the Church, through us, is not enslaving the artist and debasing his art. If we conceive of works of art as utilitarian, demanding that they favor a special mode of piety which we consider to be the right one, we shall only drive our artists out of the Church. If our principal preoccupation with art is either to hand on dreams that have been dreamed in the past or to shock the mass of the people, if in fact we think of the Church as just another political party or just another sect whose human glory we must achieve by human means, we shall drive the artist away.

Jean Cassou, commenting on the degrading effect that Marxism has had on art, saw no distinction between Soviet conformity and the conformity laid down, as he thought, by every sect. It was axiomatic for him that a church must be totalitarian because of its primary preoccupation with power. The thing such power most detests is independent creative activity. A church is, he said, a closed world in which thought can only go round and round the same old circumference.[11]

If we are repelled by such opinions, it is up to us to prove them false. If we are really faithful to the Spirit which we claim to be the guiding principle of our Christian life, we shall never give any artist the impression that we belong to a closed and totalitarian world. On the contrary, the artist should be able to see, through us, that the Church is the place where the noblest things in humanity can come to their full flowering. It is perfectly reasonable that there should be conflict between creative liberty and Marxist orthodoxy, but the infinite transcendence of Christian truth, together with the fact that it is bound up with everything of value in this world, gives Christian themes a special aptitude for becoming the personal property of the artist. A deep understanding of the liturgy and the contemplative orientation to which art is summoned should exclude all sentimentality, propaganda, and doctrinal pedantry from our intentions. On the propaganda question, I can do no better than quote the words of Elvire Jan, that an artist is a true Christian artist only when he seeks

[11] Jean Cassou, "La Révolution et la Vérité," Esprit, December, 1949, p. 947 .

for "a very secret transmission from his inner world to the inner world of his fellow men."[12] As Bazaine once remarked, an artist makes contact with the world in our days by means of the deepest solitude.[13]

With such an accent on solitude, detachment, and groping in the dark, one is faced with the fact that inner necessity in our time demands a certain poverty of our artists. At all times, of course, the sacred has asked for sacrifice, and in art the richer the means and the more splendid the effects, the greater was the artist's need for detachment from them. The artist's vocation today demands that he take note of the wretchedness in which most people live and of the tragic sense of life which conditions us all. By *wretchedness* I mean an excessive poverty, which is more than a lack of the goods of this world; it is something that attacks the integrity of our whole being.

The world's tragedy is one of wretchedness. Man's needs have increased in many ways as a result of new techniques and wider knowledge, and these needs are such that when they are not satisfied his standard of living is almost less than human. It is as if the body of modern man had been vastly inflated, whereas his soul, which needs a corresponding increase in its powers, is weaker than ever and unable to support the burden. Man has lost the true idea of himself and of his destiny; and the faithful who manage to convince themselves that they alone still have salvation are

[12] Elvire Jan, in *Esprit*, June, 1950.
[13] A radio broadcast in Paris, March 10, 1952.

the most obstinate in refusing to extend their love and understanding to others. Revolutions, wars, the threat of total annihilation are all signs of our deep wretchedness. We have a foretaste today of the Last Judgment. So many illusions have been shattered, and so many more, no doubt, must go the same way. But the destroying fire can at the same time enlighten. We are poor in convictions, but those we have are the stronger for being few.

In the world of art, our principal wretchedness is that of having been brought up on shams. We have the awful basilicas of Lisieux and Fatima, the colossal statues of the Our Lady with spiral staircases inside them, vast acreages of windows, which are like someone screeching out of tune at the side of the real artist who can only keep silence. Rouault did not dare paint a religious subject for years for fear that convention would be imperceptibly present from the start. Here was an "established disorder," calmly entrenched in its own falsehood. It needed real heroism if one were determined not to be irrevocably put off from the true values of the faith. At the other extreme from the wretchedness of sham and ostentation, there is, let us not forget, a spirit of poverty, apparent in art as in religion, which really loves the poverty of the Gospel and prefers the simple to the ostentatious. It shuns any easy, sentimental sublimity as well as that deceptive depth of feeling which is in fact only skin deep. In this world of revolution, the destinies of man and of the Church both converge on a spiritual poverty, which simplifies and purifies *inter alia* the authentic materials of art. Art must seek out what is indispensable; all the rest is false and superficial. One might even ask if anything can be sacred if it is not fraught with genuine poverty. Our churches with their bare walls and unadorned roofs may yet teach the world that what is essential to man is little enough.

The pursuit of spiritual poverty has been the major venture of art since the time of Delacroix, Corot, and Daumier, and increasingly so since the impressionists, Cézanne, and Van Gogh. Here was a movement that tore art away from every value alien to it, and exalted the true values in all their simplicity. Having done away with imitation of the antique, with formulas of style, rhetoric, and so on, the artist could be forced to invent his art again in each new work. The artist is a poor man in front of his task now. He has to begin with nothing, in the very catacombs of art.

Confronted by a despairing civilization, Christian artists were exhorted by Pius XII to make the reflection of beauty and the divine light smile on this earth, on the face of humanity; by helping man love everything true and pure, just and lovable, the artist would lead him on to peace.[14] It is impossible for the artist not to be affected by a tragic sense of life, and yet he has to try, in some way, to celebrate the glory of Christ. The solution can only come from a quality of the artist's soul, for on the superficial level there is no reconciliation between tragedy and glory. In art, however deeply tragedy may be felt, it is bound to appear superficial if it is not transposed to a higher level. Even when a work of

[14] Pius XII, discourse of September 4, 1950.

art is fundamentally a reaction of disgust or an admission of fear, it is still at least the beginning of salvation. To face facts, to accept the truth, is a saving experience. It delivers us from our illusions, and helps us overcome them.

Only God understands fully what human distress is, and when we experience distress only the divine Word of God can express it fully. A number of artists have spontaneously entered the region of Job and the Apocalypse. The strongest images of suffering are those of Christ crucified and the *Mater dolorosa*. These two evocations can express the sufferings of any age. Calvary, the descent from the cross, the flagellation, the stations of the cross, and the catastrophic events of the Apocalypse are again themes with which many artists find themselves in accord. But it is worth asking whether these artists all realize what is Christian about the truths these images express. Just as their sense of the tragic does not have the artistic power to create great works, so does it lack a truly supernatural dimension. And this supernatural dimension in no sense palliates human tragedy, but rather takes it over into the divine sphere and into the peace of God.

It would be impossible to paint a Christ on the cross that was too tragic, but the really important fact is that Christ, by his passion and death, has triumphed over death and suffering. A work that fails to show this, one that offers the mystery of salvation as despair pure and simple, is not Christian, or is only Christian in a reverse form. "I can't help it," wrote André Marchand, "if Christ for me is someone from Dachau, some twentieth-century man who has been humiliated, insulted, victimized, tracked to death or burned alive. . . ."[15] This painter is closer to the truth than he thinks: the Man of Sorrows has borne all human suffering, so that we can recognize in the face of every sufferer what the face of Christ must have been. But it is obvious that Marchand has not perceived the essential spirit of the Gospel; he goes on to suggest that had Christ lived today, his whip of cords would have been a box of dynamite to blow up the manufacturers of long-range heavy bombers. This is typical of man's inability to see what Christ meant by his refusal to call legions of angels to his help, and it is the key to such pessimistic questions as, "What is man doing on this earth anyway? What is any of us likely to achieve besides failure and disappointment?" But Christ was not a failure. Faith reveals to us that although he appeared to be a failure, God was triumphant. How art can express what faith reveals to us, I cannot begin to suggest. Perhaps it is best, in an age in which all roads seem to lead to despair, for the artist to curb his attraction to tragic themes, at least in work designed for the Church. Let him leave them alone until, as Matisse said, he can paint them blindfolded. Here again, we must accept the fact of our poverty.

A sacred work, as we have already observed, must be created in the depths of the artist's soul. It demands that suffering be transmuted by some inner alchemic process of the artist's, as I well remember Manessier saying once when we were talking about Fra Angelico and the peace and gentleness with which all his works are imbued:

[15] André Marchand, in *Cahiers de l'Art Sacré*, no. 7 (1946), pp. 19–20.

Few men have ever really achieved that state of peace. One would need to be saturated in it. Fra Angelico admitted that he knew this peace, although he never looked for it, never particularly wished for it, perhaps. In every artist you can see the effort to achieve the ideal, but mere effort and desire are not enough. It is this insufficiency that is pathetic and crucifying in the work of artists. But Fra Angelico had peace in him as if it were something inborn. There are few ways of expressing this peace, but it can be dishonestly imitated.

We live in an essentially tragic period, and this makes us tragic. As artists, we could not pass on this message if we had refused to accept it ourselves. But we know that the human sense of tragedy can very well coincide with the peace of God, by means of true, inner Christian living. In our living union with Christ today we can find real possibilities for a virile Christian art.[16]

Once again, our conclusion is that we must accept poverty. On one side, there is material and moral wretchedness, and on the other, spiritual poverty. The artist finds that the clergy and the faithful count on him to disguise their suspicions of decline by magnifying the little prestige they have left. But one must accept this poverty, and by following the little insights we are sure of, we have discovered more possibilities than we had perhaps suspected. The contemporary artist is rich in poor men's wealth. We have works of great talent (small-scale or large-scale, it makes no difference), works in which one feels that the artist is absolutely sure of what he is doing, and that he has put himself utterly into his work. We have the artists today to carry out poor men's commissions.

Such works are not numerous, and they are infinitely outnumbered by an abundance of mediocre works designed for

[16] Quoted in *Cahiers de l'Art Sacré*, no. 8 (1946), pp. 19–20.

popular pious taste to recall the splendors of an age no longer our own. Whether we think of the human context in which religious art is created—the economic, moral, and psychological structure of our society, or of the present condition of art—its intrinsic data, its corruption when it tries to play at being traditional, the fact that only when it is poor can it produce anything of worth—the same decision always confronts us: God or mammon?

10

The Non-Christian Artist in the Service of the Church

Among the most interesting questions arising from the previous discussion are three which we will now consider in turn. First, what are the chances of a non-Christian artist's producing work suitable for a church? Second, is there a place for nonobjective art in church? Third, what use can church architecture make of present-day building techniques?

The first question is an important one because at the moment some of our best artists are outside the Church, and even hostile to it. And when it is suggested that these artists should be commissioned for church decoration, a common Catholic reaction is to consider them as complete outsiders whose work, of whatever kind it may be, must be rigidly barred from churches.

Joseph Samson's answer to the problem is to consider it from the point of view of the works produced rather than to generalize about the unsuitability of non-Christian artists or argue from a determined notion of faith as a *sine qua non* of acceptance by the Church. If, he claims, a work is Christian in *tone*, it qualifies for acceptance by the Church, since this proves that there is sufficient faith in the artist who produced it.[1] This is a very reasonable approach, if only because we have plenty of good Christian work by non-Christian artists on which to base our judgment.

Of all the pictures of St. Francis de Sales, none captures the saint's spirit in quite the way that Bonnard's has. Whatever criticism we may have of Lurçat's tapestries, he has undeniably helped produce something at Assy just as sacred as anything left us by the Middle Ages. Léger's mosaic on the façade of this same church, in which we can all find minor faults, has the immediate effect of breaking off our contact with the everyday world, calling on us to transcend it, as everything truly sacred must. Then we have the windows at Audincourt, also by Léger, which have been called "some of the most overpowering work that Christian art has given us for five centuries."[2] The works speak for themselves. Matisse's chapel at Vence has such an atmosphere in it that priests saying mass there have remarked that they have not offered the sacrifice with more fervor since their ordination.

Therefore, it seems only reasonable to admit that the non-Christian artist can give us works of true magnificence which amply fulfill their function in the church—by which we mean the atmosphere they create for the faithful who are preparing to take part in the mass. This seems infinitely more constructive than decreeing from the start that no

[1] Joseph Samson, *Musique et Vie intérieure* (Paris: La Colombe, 1951), pp. 236 ff. When Matisse was asked whether an artist with no religion could produce a sacred work, he replied, "You can only tell by considering the work. Does it induce a mood of calm and recollection?"

[2] Jean Bazaine, in *La Croix*, May 14, 1952.

"unbeliever" will be allowed to create a work of art for the Church. However, it is not enough to prove that someone else can walk by walking ourselves. We have to show how it is possible, and to admit the complexity of the problem involved. The answer is unlikely to be a simple one. All I can do, after having thought the matter over for some twenty-five years, is offer some suggestions.

Since our opponents pose the problem in the first place, let us first take the arguments against the non-Christian artist's working for the Church. They maintain, for instance, that a sacred work can only be produced by someone who qualifies to do so by having the faith. "For he who comes to God must believe that God exists. . . ."[3] And of course whoever wishes to bring others to God by his work, which is a little share in the opus Dei, must certainly have faith. Fra Angelico said that to paint the things of Christ one must live with Christ, and this must be understood at its deepest level, at the level of the Christian mystery the painter was presupposing: Christ's mysterious alliance with men which the arts as the "noble handmaids of the liturgy" celebrate.

To correspond to the celebration of the liturgy, there must be an inner celebration of the heart which comes from a sincere faith. It would be a kind of sacrilege to entrust any part of the sacred act with which God is worshiped to people who make an open profession of their materialism.

This objection has its roots in a genuinely traditional outlook. We cannot have the substance of the invisible world which the liturgy makes present to us without faith. This applies not only to the non-Christian artist but also to the

[3] Heb. 11:6.

Catholic clergy and laity who may overlook it. We are only just beginning to realize how necessary it is for us to live by faith in order to share fully in the liturgy, and it is precisely this fact, now gradually dawning in people's minds again, which tends to exclude the non-Christian artist.

The artist without faith cannot be involved in his creation insofar as it is supposed to be Christian. For him, the fact that his work is destined for a religious use or that his theme is religious is only a side issue. The meaning he gives his work will only coincide accidentally with the meaning the Church wants it to have. As I said before, the contemporary artist is someone who undergoes artistic creation rather than wills it. And this can mean that the non-Christian artist, unprotected by faith, is more or less the victim of an outlook which is spiritually and morally dangerous. The arts today tend to neglect our higher feelings, almost as if these could only give rise to a literature and art of poor quality. As a young man, Delacroix felt the urge to bring out the dark side of human nature, and since then religious art has often overemphasized the sinful, the sordid, and the tragic. Without faith, despair and many other deviations are almost inevitable. Some of our contemporaries have indeed incorporated something decidedly perverted into their treatment of religious subjects. St. Peter's words are curiously apt in this connection: "Be sober, be watchful! . . . Resist, steadfast in the faith. . . ."[4]

To this we must add the fact that ours is not a Christian century. Artists at other times could be carried along by a

[4] I Pet. 5:8–9.

religious current they did not fully share and produce genuinely sacred works, but in the words of Jean de Fabrègues, "Non-Christian artists may well produce works that are of interest to Christians, but it is very unlikely that their work could nourish Christian faith or be any sort of support or inspiration to Christians in general."[5]

An objection formulated by Henri Charlier is based on the fact that the Christian religion is supernatural. Faith is not of the natural order. To understand the Christian mysteries, to know Christ, one must live by faith. The supernatural experience of grace is an absolute necessity, without which not even the best will or the most detailed explanations can avail anything. Without this experience, the artist can only be guided basically by his feelings and (more disastrously, of course) by his sentimentality.[6]

Sincerity is so essential that no one without faith should be allowed to paint for the Church. Picasso once said that since a woman never smokes a pipe, a woman painter has no business painting a pipe.[7] He would certainly look askance at the current practice of accepting militant Communists as religious painters.

All these reasons against employing the non-Christian artist have seemed so extremely convincing that they have colored the vision of their protagonists in advance. When they saw the tapestry at Assy, they saw it as the triumph of the Beast in the sanctuary; the mosaic was, to them, only

[5] Jean de Fabrègues, in *La France Catholique*, August 10, 1951.
[6] Henri Charlier, in *Écrits de Paris*, September, 1951, pp. 51–52, and a contribution to *Problèmes de l'Art Sacré* (1952), p. 141.
[7] Cited by Kahnweiler, in the issue "*Picasso à Vallauris*," of *Verve*, 1951.

suitable for a night-club entrance, and the glorious face of
Our Lady in its center, they said, had an imbecile look; the
chapel at Vence was a work of pure sensuality. They even
said these works represented a "technique of degradation"
engineered by Moscow.[8]

Let us now look at some of the arguments for the other
side, beginning with the very sensible one that can be drawn
from the work of artists who profess the Christian faith. We
must admit, if we examine their work, that they do not give
a very exciting impression of the Christian faith. It soon
becomes apparent that the arguments regarding the non-
Christian artist are on two different levels. On one side it
may be argued that faith, in the abstract, is the essential
issue. On the other side are those who consider faith not as
an abstraction but as a state of things manifested here and
now. It is all very well to envisage faith as living, balanced,
integrated, and soundly equipped for correcting even any
deviations in an artist's feelings. But in practice, what do
we find? What is the faith of our contemporaries, in fact?
And what is that faith really capable of?

If we are honest, we must admit that the faith of the
present day is riddled with ignorance, error, and vague,
muddled thinking.[9] Instead of grasping the invisible world
boldly and bringing it to us with absolute conviction, today's faith appears as a rather negative, servile form of obedience, preoccupied essentially with not going against what

[8] L. Jourdain, in *Pensée Catholique*, July, 1952.
[9] See Père Paissac, "L'Athéisme des Chrétiens," *Supplément de
la Vie Spirituelle*, May 15, 1947.

the Church teaches. It is theoretical, and yet it is far from finding a meeting ground with current ways of thinking, even on the theoretical plane. Its attempts to provide artistic themes savor too much of system and the catechism. The artists who profess Christianity are, as often as not, the most sentimental. It is not surprising if the works that the pious artist produces for pious people manifest clearly the dull, dispirited devotion that belongs to the common faith of many today. This judgment is not made of people's inner lives, of course, but simply of the external manifestations of their lives. All sorts of historical factors are involved, and they explain how a real, heroic faith could—as in the case of St. Theresa of Lisieux—be inextricably bound up with the most appalling mawkishness.

We may talk all we want to about art on the ideal level, but when we examine the valid works we have today and the conditions of their achievement, we cannot overlook facts. We have to conclude that in certain cases a "non-Christian" will have a deeper, more genuine, and more effective feeling for the theme or function of a work than will a "Christian." The abstract notions of faith and unbelief are of little avail. And even when the outward manifestation of the artist's faith is beyond reproach and has no ill effect on his creative expression, he is still likely to be dominated by the idealistic notion of the supremacy of faith over all the means at his disposal, and thus committed to translating the ideal world into works of art. This, as Bazaine said, is the reason the artists who produce "religious art" so often fail in their task. To begin with an act of faith and then adapt a given reality of ordinary life to it is to bring together two independent entities which will never meet.[10] This is the reason why all "committed" art fails, as we have already observed. When bound to such a scheme, art cannot take its normal course. It is artificially manipulated for the good of the cause. The artists who engage in such activity are betraying that cause whenever they set out to serve it.

Whereas the faith of many Christian artists has absolutely no effect on their work, there are nonbelievers whose Christian reaction to Christian themes is very striking indeed, just as we find far higher religious ideals among some non-Catholics than among some Catholics. Instead of dull conformity, we find the pure spontaneity of unerring instinct. Therefore, it may well be argued, let the Church profit by the work of the unbeliever when it is clearly the product of his whole being, fundamentally attuned to the realities of our faith. How often we find among such artists a truly vital aspiration toward the sacred, far more intense and demanding than is found among many Christians!

A further argument, often pushed rather too far, follows the conception advanced by the German Romantics and Kierkegaard, of the "ironic" character of art. The plastic arts, it is agreed, are wholly inadequate to depict supernatural mysteries. Therefore, the imagination of the artist is a kind of substitute for faith, and the nonbeliever can thus produce valid work for the Church. Art is the opposite of life, in the sense that it follows the artist's inner voice in order to produce an expression, and nothing more.

[10] Jean Bazaine, Notes sur la Peinture d'Aujourd'hui (Paris: Fleury, 1948), p. 59.

Another argument is that art is merely decorative (here the Classical and Baroque traditions influence the theory) and need not be taken too seriously. True faith is unnecessary when art is a matter of adaptations and suitabilities. A work of art, for many critics, is sufficiently sacred if it is good painting or sculpture. There is, for them, no specifically Christian or sacred art. Art is only Christian or sacred when it submits to laws of appropriateness for its destined place. Any gifted, intelligent, sensitive artist can appreciate what is fitting, and be sufficiently influenced by it to produce the work required. This is a superficial conception, perhaps, but it does at least present a serious view of art, although the value offered is only that of a work honestly executed. Every good painting, Michelangelo said, is noble and devotional in itself[11] and therefore is able to honor God, whether or not the artist is a believer.

Then there are those who feel that the inner flame of the artist is necessarily sacred of its nature. If inspiration is profound, the work of art is *ipso facto* religious and therefore worthy of being put in a church. This is a sufficient faith, they say; supernatural faith is not essential.

The principal argument is closely akin to this last one, and may easily be confused with it. The difference between the two is that the argument above is purely naturalistic; its proponents are not concerned with supernatural faith, and

[11] See Chapter 1, footnote 35. Michelangelo can also be quoted as giving a contrary opinion, when he said that it is not enough for a painter to be merely a good painter when he is "imitating the venerable image of Our Lord." He must also be a good man, and if possible a saint, so that the Holy Spirit of God may inspire his understanding.

so its necessity does not arise for them. But those who maintain the line of argument we will consider next state quite clearly that supernatural faith is the more or less immediate principle in virtue of which a work will be worthy of the Church. What they ask of the unbelieving artist, and what they find in him, is the aptitude to be somehow affected by the living faith of the Church. This aptitude is found precisely in the "inner flame," the depth of the artist's inspiration.

With this in mind, Père Couturier wrote, "Every great artist is intuitive. This is almost always enough."[12] And again:

Genius does not give a man faith, but there is too great an analogy between mystical inspiration and the inspiration of great heroes and artists for there not to be a prejudice in artists' favor from the outset. One must always be prepared to find genius in a work of art, Delacroix said. Every real artist is inspired. By nature and by temperament, he is predisposed to receive spiritual intuitions—why not also, then, to receive that Breath who breathes where he will?[13]

If this is a valid argument, it can cover a wide field. At first sight, it would appear to concern only great artists; but in fact any sort of artistic genius, small or great, can perceive and express the realities embodied in the message of the true faith as soon as that message is properly conveyed to him. The artist becomes for a moment, as Joseph Samson

[12] Père Couturier, in the Swiss review Werk, no. 4 (1949), p. 120.

[13] Père Couturier, in L'Art Sacré, September–October, 1950, pp. 17–18.

has put it, what he has been told or what he has told himself to say. The subject inspires him and confers its own qualities on him. The essence of genius is the gift of being able to receive, to welcome, to incorporate into oneself a message from outside. A painter who has loved the forms of fruit that went into his still life can love the straw, the crib, the Nativity scene with Our Lord and his mother, Joseph, the ox and the ass. Moreover, he loves all that these things represent for others and for himself. He may be surprised that he loves thus, as if he had acquired a new and unfamiliar tone of voice he cannot at first recognize as his own. How has this happened? What is the answer, the reason? If the appeal of these things comes from a source whose existence he had hitherto not suspected, that does not prevent him from giving his response in a way that is worthy of the subject he has suddenly come to love.[14]

It is not so much the presence or absence of faith that we can discern in works of art as the precise qualities of that faith or the particular degree in which it is insufficient. This amounts to saying that we cannot tell whether it is faith that is involved or some substitute for faith. For the Christian artist, faith makes him sensitive to the supernatural as well as to all the data of everyday life. If an artist does not have faith, he cannot be completely attuned to the whole Christian outlook, but he will be partially attuned, in certain tendencies and on certain points. Theoretically, one could say that the Christian artist is like a wireless receiver that can pick up all wavelengths, whereas the non-Christian can

[14] Samson, op. cit., pp. 236–247.

receive only a few. But in practice, all artists, whether Christian or otherwise, tend to be much the same. The area in which they partake of the *sensus Ecclesiae* seems to be rather limited for both.

An artist finds perceptible equivalents for the mysterious facts of faith; and as far as this goes, there seems to be very little difference between what the Christian and the non-Christian can find. There is, in other words, hardly any difference at this stage between real faith and its substitutes or equivalents. What difference is there, after all, between actual faith in the mysteries of Christianity and a vivid comprehension of them without actual belief? The only difference is an assent which does not affect this comprehension of the mysteries, at least in their material expression in art. Therefore, it is almost impossible to say whether any artist judged by his work alone has or has not true faith. It is probably better to leave such judgments to God.

Supernatural faith and the nonbelieving artist's substitute for faith are both a share in the faith of the Church. Real faith and substitute faith function in the sphere of art in the same way. Both the believer and the unbeliever, in virtue of some vital attraction to a point of faith, are open to the Church's teaching on that point. Normally, of course, the believer is privileged in his understanding, but here again it is impossible to generalize, for it is spiritual sensitivity more than faith that influences the artist's reaction and is expressed in plastic form.

In either case, the extreme complexity of our present problems breaks down the accepted theory that supernatural faith in the artist affects the sacred value of his work. Of course, all works of sacred art are sacred in virtue only of the supernatural faith by which the Church lives, but it is perfectly possible that a substitute for faith in one artist's soul can achieve more than the supernatural faith of another. And we may well find many cases of this anomaly; but these will serve as exceptions that prove the rule, for a substitute for faith still only acts in accordance with the demands of faith.

At this juncture we can perhaps rectify whatever was too partial in our two opposing views, and this will help us at the same time to make one or two doctrinal points clear.

For those who deny that an unbeliever can produce a work of sacred art, I would like to suggest that strictly speaking sacred art only requires a sacred character of the actual artistic creation, of the artist's exercise of his art. The most truly sacred artist in the Church, I would say, is the one who puts the most sacred quality in the forms of his creation. Artists who profess to be materialists can very well be the best equipped for certain tasks in the Church. A true artist is not a logician. His apparent materialism may quite conceivably be the result of a thirst for justice or an extreme altruism. Each case must be considered on its own merits, and of course the whole question would be unthinkable in a really Christian society. But society today is not Christian, and we have to take the world as it comes.

Then again, just as every preacher should be able to preach about any given point of doctrine, any Christian artist should be able (one might think) to paint any given subject. But this is simply not the case. The non-Christian artist may feel the subject much more strongly, and it is foolish to claim that for the non-Christian the sacred subject is only a side issue. A woman does not smoke a pipe; we grant that with Picasso, but an artist without actual faith can still be in strong communion with many realities of the supernatural world. To say that his interest is only sentimental is another superficial judgment. The analogy between the natural and the supernatural, the spirit's power of rising from this world to the supernatural, the working of actual graces in the soul, all these go well beyond the realm of sentiment. And it is evident, if we examine their work, that artists of today are far from sentimental in their treatment of sacred themes. On the contrary, they react against sentimentality very strongly.

It seems, then, that non-Christian artists should be allowed to work for the Church. The imaginative intuition must be understood as being a sort of artistic faith which is so deeply rooted in the creator's soul that it is present in all his powers. The theme of a work, as Verdi said, becomes part of his blood.[15] There is hardly any need to add that even when one can count on genius, one cannot expect any single artist to be capable of everything. As we shall see in a later chapter, the Abbé Devémy and the priest responsible for the church at Assy brought in "unbelievers" but each one was invited to do just what he seemed best fitted to do.

[15] Quoted by M. Moré in *Dieu Vivant*, no. 20, p. 124.

Finally, there is again the note of poverty to consider. If the unbelievers are poor, they are magnificently poor. They can give back to the Church the true riches of Christ. But what they give back to the Church they have only received from the faith of Christ in the first place.

11

Whatever our personal opinion may be on the subject of nonrepresentational art, it is quite obviously something more than a passing phase. Many artists—indeed, some of the greatest in our time—say that they have been led to produce nonobjective works simply because that was the way their development lay. Sometimes the driving force of this tendency toward the abstract has led them to paint religious subjects. It could also be that their need for the sacred element in art has been the chief reason for their producing nonrepresentational works. Many people tend to think of a church as the atmosphere in which abstract art may best flourish, and it is certainly true that the field of religious art reveals all the most acute problems of painting and sculpture at the present time.

Inevitably, nonrepresentational art has come in for a great deal of criticism from all quarters, but after having studied the arguments brought against it over the last eight years, I should say that all the objections can be summed up in the objections we will consider throughout this chapter.

Let us take first of all the objection that nonrepresentational art is the result of a system which is both artificial and oversimplified and which has declared itself the enemy of all art forms with which we have hitherto been familiar. Now, I will not deny that some of the more fanatic abstract artists have made this their manifesto, but it would certainly be unwise to condemn out of hand the nonrepresentational works that deserve our consideration quite independently of the theories that discredit them. Unfortunately, the discussion has been complicated from the beginning by the prejudices of the opposing parties. There is obviously no theoretical manifesto behind the work of Bazaine and Manessier, whose art appears to be simply a very deep communion with all living things. Their work provides just two cases among many of the artist's being the first to be astonished at what his inner voice has led him to create. Genuine theories about abstract art are always the fruit of reflection on the artist's own experience, and what is perhaps even more striking, the theories apply to representational and nonrepresentational art equally well. These theories in no way militate against a possible return to representational art.

The next objection comes from the many people who want to know, "What is it?" when they see anything new. Most of us want to explain everything we see, and when we are in the habit of looking for familiar shapes even in the clouds, our reaction to almost any painting is likely to be, "What is it meant to be?" It would be unnatural to do otherwise, of course, and that is why for most of us there is something unsatisfying in looking at mere splashes of color.

In theory, at least, we can concede that the most satisfactory art form is the one that offers something of interest to the viewer's whole personality, particularly to his mind. Common sense likes to recognize familiar objects in works of art. But if the viewer has any visual sensitivity, his appreciation is not heightened by the completeness of the objects or their appeal to common sense. The quality of the work may gain in his eyes from a more pronounced bias or a more specialized development.

In any case, the greatness of man does not lie exclusively in his reason but rather in the human spirit taken in its entirety. Discursive reasoning is not the only activity of the spirit. Admittedly, the human spirit is a rational entity, but the value of our reasoning depends on intuitions which we need not mistrust since they do possess a certain purity. The plastic arts must be apprehended above all by what one might call a simple intuition. This probably sounds as if one were claiming quasi-angelic powers, but it is perfectly true that we have something in us of the type of perception which the angels possess by nature. It is not necessary to reason about the painting and sculpture we see; all we need do is look at it. When the work of art is a genuine product of the artist's soul, it is our artistic awareness that is called into play, not a pure knowledge of truth or, for that matter, the mere satisfaction of the senses. There can be spiritual qualities about every tone of color, every stroke of the brush, and these awaken the spirit of anyone who really contemplates a work of art. A work of art should draw us to the pure contemplation of itself. It is all the better if we have no grounds for the satisfaction of our common sense, no starting points for more or less irrelevant trains of thought.

Whether we consider popular realism from the human point of view or from that of artistic quality, we are bound to admit that it is a degradation, however elevated its inspiration may originally have been. Artists of today are trying to come to grips with the full impact of human reality, and it is precisely such nonrepresentational artists as Bazaine and Manessier who have expressed this most intensely. The mere representation of appearances counts for nothing, they say. These artists have put their finger on a need, their own and every man's, for an inner world, without which the outer world cannot be built anew. This is the world which is revealed in their work, the inner world which is the productive force that communicates itself through what they give us. And since there is a sympathy between all inner worlds, our own is opened up to us more fully through the sight of their richer one. Of course, anyone who denies that there is any spiritual quality in the specific means of art will probably deny that there is any communication at all. If this communication does not take place, all that is left in representational painting also is something from which all the spiritual content has been drained. The real worth of a work by Corot, Vermeer, or Titian is something that cannot be rooted in the fact that it is representational, for it lies in something much more subtle.

What we might call the human quality in art is so striking in abstract works that one can distinguish all its nuances and see clearly how great a part is contributed by the artist's heart. Manessier was perfectly right when he said, "My pictures aim to express something my own heart has experi-

enced, and not to imitate something my eyes have seen."[1]
These works disprove the common objection that abstract
art is inhuman and makes no appeal to the heart. One could
answer, in fact, excessively representational subjects stand in
the way of this appeal to the heart since they let our appreciation go no further than our eyes can see. The subject is
purely visual, and cannot be transformed into something
that the heart can accept.

Some people insist on having a recognizable subject in a
work of art. Without such a subject, their interest cannot be
held. They will give you a catalogue of all the qualities they
look for—a beautiful idea behind the work, beautiful feelings conveyed, all the eloquent details and ingenious devices
which come out in the representation of a recognizable subject. In abstract art, they will say, there is nothing to get
hold of because none of these qualities is apparent. But the
answer to these people is that none of the qualities they
expect to find belong to the sphere of painting or sculpture.
When they make such judgments as these, the values that
influence them are really literary ones. Such values have
always enhanced the work of art when the creative imagination of the artist was genuinely inspired by them, but the
subject matter alone can never provide the total value of a
picture or a piece of sculpture. Nowadays, indeed, our best
artists tend to find the most stimulating subjects for their
work in a theme, something at once spiritual and perceptible. They would appear to find this far more satisfying
than the kind of subject that can be rationally explained.
The important point to bear in mind concerning this sort

[1] Quoted in René Huyghe, *La Peinture contemporaine.*

of objection is that most of the public are likely to feel quite lost when confronted with a work of art in which no subject is recognizable, and abstract art is therefore bound to meet with much misunderstanding and abuse.

Although there are large numbers of people today whose demands are not quite so exacting in the matter of a recognizable subject, nonetheless most people still prefer to be able to see something with which experience has made them familiar. They feel that the value of a work must depend on its value as a representation of life. Sometimes they even go so far as to say that if there is no actual reference to visible nature, then the picture contains nothing by which to judge its pictorial or plastic values. Their criteria are a faithful reproduction of nature or a more or less free interpretation of it. If the object is not recognizable, whether it be imitated or interpreted in paint or clay, how can one judge the merits of the work? Old maxims are constantly bandied about: "Art is the splendor of Truth"; "Art imitates nature."

When there are no natural forms to be identified in a painting, people start exclaiming that art is being prostituted—always on the assumption that the dependence of art on nature is the dependence of a copy on a model. All the principles of traditional esthetics are brought in to demonstrate conclusively that nonrepresentational art is something metaphysically monstrous. This happens particularly in ecclesiastical circles. It has been solemnly asserted, "This art is not art at all, for it lacks unity, clarity, harmony, and splendor." This is true only if by "clarity" we understand no more than straightforward representation, by "unity" a composition in the accepted mode, by "harmony" the choice of models, and by "splendor" (one can well imagine) classic and even academic attitudes. But precisely the art detached from the pursuit of figure delineation makes us see that clarity, unity, harmony, and splendor are quite independent of the slavish imitation of appearances.

One cannot help marveling that there are disciples of St. Thomas Aquinas who deny this, for by doing so they compromise their own authority as well as St. Thomas's teaching. Nothing in the sphere of art can possess more clarity, more harmony and unity, more splendor than a work that is the outcome of contemplation; and contemplation is not inextricably bound to the physical aspect of things. The "splendor of truth" in a work of art consists of the artist's faithful expression of his inner world, and this expression is brought to life through his contemplation and absorption of created beauty.

Art certainly "imitates nature," but as we have already seen, if we limit this principle to realism and nothing more, then we are falsifying the meaning this principle originally had. Braque's words are faithful to that original meaning: "I do not try to copy nature. I try to be in union with nature." The techniques that art involves (for instance, proportion, rhythm, and color harmony in painting) are sufficiently determined to produce works which have an inner coherence. Quite independently of any reference to the visible world, we can judge a nonrepresentational work of art on its merits as a plastic and pictorial achievement. Such an achievement is sufficient to define it as a work of art. Objections are not wanting, however, to such an ex-

planation. Some will insist that we are contradicting ourselves when we say there is something to be perceived in a
work of art which lacks any reference to nature. Then there
are those who are indignant that the artist should lay claim
to any creative activity at all. And others claim that such a
conception of art as I have put forward is suitable to music
but not the visual arts.

Is there, in fact, a contradiction involved when an artist
claims to imitate the activities of nature while detaching
himself from the forms and appearances in which these activities are embodied? It is through these appearances, many
people say, that we find out how nature works; what can be
valid about any work that overlooks them? Here we are
certainly at the root of the problem, but all we can do is appeal to the eye itself. Some eyes are never opened; these are
the eyes that can never recognize painting as something
which is quite as enchanting and quite as revealing as any
spectacle that nature has to offer, and which can be contemplated in just the same way as nature. Only the seeing eye
can realize that there is no contradiction between imitating
nature in its activities and discarding natural forms. Everything here is happening in the creative imagination.

But in fact it is not the artist who claims to imitate nature in its activities but the philosopher in that artist, who
reflects on what the artist has done and puts the process
into words. The artist only expresses what he experiences,
and his experience is that of a microcosm in which the
whole cosmos has repercussions. In the creative imagination emotion and its expression become one. While the
artist is elaborating a composition, he will not consciously

detach himself from all immediate reference to nature's appearances, but if he is really sensitive, it will be nature itself that awakens and guides his imagination. It is the same for those who look at the picture with a seeing eye; their senses, their imagination, and their poetic appreciation, already developed by contemplating the beauty of the world of nature, will be equally delighted by the artist's picture.

The fundamental argument is not between representational and nonrepresentational painting but between artists who, whether they paint abstractly or representationally, either work in virtue of an uninterrupted communion with the world or claim that they owe it no debt at all. The difference is an important one, and we shall have occasion to return to it.

Inevitably, of course, nonrepresentational painters are accused more often than any other modern artists of reshaping God's creation, but it is lamentable that the reproach should so often be made by the clergy. The accusation is unfounded, of course. Nonrepresentational painters are neither more nor less sacrilegious than representational painters. Art has always been held in reverence as a true creation, albeit creation in the loose sense. No human artist creates from nothing as God does. Painters whose compositions consist purely of related colors and forms are motivated neither by vaulting ambition nor by disgust for the physical aspects of creation. The whole accusation is based on such exorbitant metaphysical considerations that it goes well beyond the scope of the problem and quite beyond the aim which artists set themselves.

Nonrepresentational artists and their defenders have used comparisons with music to explain their work, but we must not understand this use of musical terminology too literally. The only reason they have had recourse to such terms is because language is inadequate for any discussion of pictorial values. Musical analogies are felt to suggest more vividly the sort of effects achieved by a painting which does not have any immediate reference to the visible world. Music provides the analogy most suitable for helping us understand the possibility of pure plastic creation and such special characteristics as its aptitude for expressing spiritual values. But the use of musical terms never implies more than an analogy.

Another common objection is that nonrepresentational painting can never be anything more than ornamental. Some claim that its use is wholly decorative and that it must therefore always belong to a lower level of art. Some critics have even said that they have nothing at all against it but would suggest that it cannot be classed as painting, that the nonrepresentational is justified only in designs for tapestries, mosaics, ceramics, or stained glass.

Here again we have to examine some facts, for we must admit that there are different levels and tendencies to be reckoned with in this art as in any other. There is a facile and decorative type of nonrepresentational art, comparable in its superficiality to dinner music. And there is nonrepresentational art which is truly great painting. It is great because it draws us into that inner world of which I have spoken repeatedly. This inner world, which some appreciate and some do not, is the central point at issue in the whole discussion. When we have come into contact with this inner world, we simply have no wish to be distracted by the unusual quality of the materials involved. The remarkable thing is that when our poet-painters like Bazaine and Manessier do produce decorative work in mosaic and stained glass, they confer even on these media the impress of their inner world. Decorative work normally tends to be dazzling, striking, provocative, and this is accentuated when the windows or mosaics are telling a narrative or using geometrical motifs; but in the hands of fine artists, mere decor becomes an inducement to contemplation because of that magical interplay of forms which is so expressive of our deepest levels of consciousness. This is why such an art form fits so beautifully into churches where the decoration becomes functional. Manessier's windows at Bréseux and Bazaine's mosaic at Audincourt, for instance, are so completely the product of the artists' contemplation and so evocative of their inner worlds that what are normally distractions become in fact a powerful means of helping us to achieve recollection.

Then there is the objection that nonrepresentational art is less difficult than representational. Here it is not at all easy to know exactly what the objectors mean. What kind of difficulty is meritorious in art? There is a certain ease of execution which springs from very arduous preparation, and there are things easily done but purposely made difficult. It is almost impossible to see the value in a criterion of difficulty, abstracted from the artist and considered in itself; such a quality can only be judged in relation to the artist. As far as art goes, the only really interesting difficulty is that of achieving values, often elementary ones, by an effort of all the artist's powers. Some people might say, when they see a particular harmony of colors or a certain rhythm of lines, "That's easy! I could have done it myself; a child could have done it!" Let me answer only that it is possible to overlook what may be a rare quality in something apparently simple.

Of course, it is perfectly true that most nonrepresentational painters would be incapable of producing a still life in the Dutch fashion or a devotional composition in the Caravaggio style. But this is not the sort of thing that interests them, simply because there are seasonal charges in art as in everything else, and today's painters do not want to produce the kind of work that belongs to another era. Supposing representational art is more difficult in itself, does that really matter? Granted that it is true, we can forget it (for all the good it may do us), turn to the artists themselves, and see what is the best they can give us. Some of them can certainly produce excellent representational works, but this is no reason why others (and some of the very best) should not give us something quite different. If we knew how to look at their work, we would find it infinitely satisfying. This should be enough to make us want to go halfway in trying to understand what they are telling us.

We must face the fact that there is a great deal of bad nonrepresentational art, but whether the amount of bad representational work is less we can hardly judge. The answer is probably that bad nonrepresentational art can deceive more people than bad representational art. I can think of several artists whose representational work is quite valueless but who have made themselves a reputation as "abstract painters." One can still recognize in their abstract work their own particular brand of mediocrity.

There is a risk for young artists who plunge right from the beginning into abstract art, especially if they do not work from nature. How many of them are working in a vacuum! If they cannot produce anything perceptible from a pot of flowers, what is the good of what they produce from their dry imagination? The pure and shining form at which non-representational art aims must come at the end of a process. No one may lay claim to it from the start. But if there is constant communion with nature, nonrepresentational art will dictate its own discipline to anyone who is both tal-ented and ready for hard training. We must not forget that representational painters have always liked to set their pic-tures upside down occasionally, just to make sure that they contained genuine pictorial quality. Nonrepresentational treatment forbids the artist to paint a flattering reproduc-tion of a recognizable form; this is an alibi many beginners hide behind. It is true, unfortunately, that the danger of anarchy and confusion has increased since the nonrepresen-tational has been accepted into the world of art, but let us be honest and admit that the values of the world of art had been debased, even lost, long before the advent of this new tendency.

Another complaint that we often hear is that the theme of a nonrepresentational work is not easily discernible. If I were not told what the picture represented, would I know, for instance, that the painting I have in front of me now is supposed to be an interpretation of the *Salve Regina*, while the one over there is inspired by the passion according to St. Matthew? Here I can merely suggest that we try to be simple in our approach to works of art, and ask of each only what it was intended to give us. Obviously, we must look to a representational painter for a picture of a choir of monks chanting the *Salve* or of episodes of the passion as they are recorded in St. Matthew's Gospel; but he will not give us precisely what we have in nonrepresentational art.

When you listen to Cistercian monks singing Compline, you are aware of a unique fusion of music and prayer. It is this same kind of subtle fusion that has determined the artist's choice of colors and harmonies, and these in turn communicate that fusion to the viewer. That is all the artist intended to do. There is no need to look for anything more than that. And if you let the painting work on you, you will agree that it is indeed full of pure, deep values, both sensible and spiritual. You would even have to agree that a representational treatment of a choir of monks would not communicate that fusion at all.

The same thing happens when one is meditating on St. Matthew's account of the passion. There is a certain spiritual reaction in the soul, and the painter perceives it in his own way. By conveying his perception in paint, he can communicate his reaction, that is to say, what goes on in his inner world, and in ours, too, as a result of this meditation. Of course, someone else might do the same by depicting a particular episode of the passion narrative. When all these explanations have been given, people may still say, "Well and good, but unless you are told that this picture is meant to be St. Matthew's account of the passion and this one the

Salve Regina, no one could possibly tell what each is!" But here again, we need to make an effort at simplicity. When we contemplate these works, their effect on us is that (over and above the impressions we perceive, and at the same time *in* and *through* these impressions) they put us in a certain state of mind. This state of mind, even of spirit, is something quite specific and yet quite difficult to express. It is not verbally communicable. It is simply the state of mind produced when we hear the *Salve* being sung by Cistercian monks, or when we meditate on certain passages of St. Matthew's narration of the passion. We may not make this identification with our unaided powers, but does that matter when the theme of the work, its spiritual reality, is effected in us by the work of art in question? The work expresses all it can to us, and that is enough.

Our present-day civilization has accustomed us to demanding and being satisfied by concepts, language, and all sorts of material qualities. These we normally substitute for spiritual realities, so that they tend to replace them completely. Thus we often seem to be out of our depth. We are lost when, without some recognizable material means, spiritual realities demand our attention. These realities must come to us not as something abstract but as something alive. They come in a form which is more perceptible to our senses and to our inner appreciation than a representational treatment of the same reality. Some kinds of nonrepresentational art find their correspondence in us as an instinctive reaction, as a need to contact the supernatural more directly.

It is still possible to insist that a sacred theme must be

treated in a way that will make it recognizable—treated, in fact, strictly according to appearance. We cannot lightly dismiss appearances, for Our Lord revealed himself to us by this means in his Incarnation. If we want to see a Nativity, a Madonna, or an *Ecce Homo*, we expect more than a theme. These are scenes that require representation. Without representation, the faithful have nothing to help their devotion, and the artist is betraying the Incarnation.

This objection can be valid in respect to certain functions of sacred art, but it does not exclude the nonrepresentational from the sanctuary or the rest of the church. If the people want a Madonna or an *Ecce Homo* or a Nativity of the type which will evoke everything relevant to the first Christmas, then obviously representational art is demanded. The representational field is the widest in the domain of Christian art, and there is every reason why this should be so. But religious art has many functions, and it would be wrong to limit it to the purely representational. The mysteries of our faith, we must not forget, are mysterious because they are of the spiritual order, and the faithful can— even want to—contemplate these mysteries as they are depicted nonobjectively. They can do so without having the scene of the mystery composed for them. Of course, even nonrepresentational painting satisfies this need very inadequately, as is true of all religious painting. Nonrepresentational painting still belongs to the domain of the senses and emotions, which it can enhance only in its own way. It is still in the sphere of the Incarnation, and this sphere must not be limited to include simply a certain number of proportions and techniques and materials. If it is thus limited, we get the type of religious painting that tries to be absolutely exact in every feature of local color and costume and is executed with the minutest attention to irrelevant details. Certainly, one cannot condemn such exactitude out of hand. A genius may be able to give it a spiritual value. But we may be suspicious about the probable consequences of such an approach. We would like to see the same allowance made for nonrepresentational work, of the type which evokes directly and purely the intense love that a contemplative finds in the Christian mysteries. Manessier's "Passion According to St. Matthew,"[2] for instance, has grown on many people through the sheer simplicity and directness of its colors. The picture invites us to contemplate Our Lord in his passion, and our contemplation is penetrated by it and bound up in it. This is a true "composition of place," if we are sufficiently simple and sensitive to realize it. The blood and fire of Manessier's composition in red give us some communion with the suffering soul of Christ and some awareness of the intensity of his glory, which only faith can help us to perceive. A consuming fire is there which could be divine and human love at the same time: this is the essence of the mystery, and we experience it in this painting in a way that is unique.

Only one difficulty is really serious, and it has occurred in each of the objections raised thus far. It is the objection that nonrepresentational art is not easy to appreciate. It goes contrary to our habitual notions of pictorial and plastic

[2] Manessier's "Passion According to St. Matthew" is in the Couvent de Saint-Jacques in Paris.

values. When we see a painting or a piece of sculpture, some people argue, we do not look at it; we examine it to see what it represents. Nonrepresentational art could not be a means for any large-scale communion between men. The more we praise the quality of our best nonrepresentational work, the more we emphasize the factors that make the appreciation of this sort of art the prerogative of an elite. Very few people do appreciate the qualities of painters like Manessier, and these qualities are being developed at the expense of the accepted means of expression. The sensitivities of different artists are given full scope for exaggeration and seem to offer the viewer nothing but a frenzy of individualism.

There is no need to point out how serious this matter is when a work of art claims to have some function in the worship of the Church, because before all else Christianity in worship is something essentially communal. It must give priority to the least of the brethren. We have spoken of prejudices, but the fact that they are prejudices is secondary to the fact that they are a very real condition that must be taken into consideration. They are a warning to us to be very prudent. No problem is raised by a privately owned picture, but only by those which become public property. However, when a nonrepresentational work of art is offered to the public, it is interesting to see that once they have recovered from their first reactions, people take more easily to the completely nonrepresentational than they do to the type of art that merely distorts appearances. It has often never occurred to such people that a painting may represent *nothing.* But this being the case, why may they not just stand in front of it and look at it, as they might stand and look at the sea or the sunset?

When we have removed all these difficulties, we can also contemplate the works themselves, just as they are. But there are still several sides to the question of nonrepresentational art that give us food for thought. First of all, there is the problem of its significance in the historical evolution of art. Then there is the nature, and also the purpose, of this "inner world" which it claims for its justification. And as a consequence of this, we have to consider its place in religious art.

Regarding nonrepresentational art and its role in the world today, we might be tempted to agree with the following viewpoint, which seems penetrating and sound. Art, so this explanation goes, imitates nature in nature's own activity. In our own day, we are discovering that nature's activity is far more complex than anything that a superficial observation could reveal. If modern art tends then to ignore the externals of nature's activity, it is only keeping pace with the rest of our knowledge. We are perfectly aware now that almost nothing is as we tend to picture it, whether we are considering the structure of matter, vegetable or animal life, the heavenly bodies, or the soul.

Although there is something that seems very deep about such a reflection as this, if we examine rather the immediate data of our experience we shall perhaps reach more valuable conclusions.

Artists will always be concerned with what their senses contact—their sensual experience, in other words. The conclusions of science have little effect on the artist, particularly when they are so far removed from ordinary experience that the imagination has nothing to work on. I do not believe that nonrepresentational art is to representational art what the world of Einstein, de Broglie, Cuénot, or Freud is to the world of common sense. The only connection I can see is that the way we look at things has been conditioned to a certain extent by their theories, which in a popular form are now everyone's property. But artists have always transcended the world of appearances. They have always had their own special vision to put in the place of any utilitarian outlook on life. Their inner world is the one which spirit and feelings together bring about, as they instinctively imitate the way nature works. The artistic instinct is so conditioned nowadays that it knows something of the vast scale on which nature works, and artists therefore have a deepened sense of mystery, a greater need to transcend limitations, a greater thirst for freedom. But all this explains very little about nonrepresentational art.

It is also unwise to exaggerate the importance of social conditions in the artist's reactions, which are, however, always roused by the cause of liberty and by any increase of oppression in society. Nonrepresentational art certainly expresses one extreme of liberty. At the same time, one can go to the other extreme in representational art, as Picasso has shown us. The oppressive thing about our present-day world is not the visible appearance of nature. Today, more than ever, the artist has made himself free, and has made us free too, by transfiguring these appearances. Representational and nonrepresentational artists would both applaud these words of Pius XII: "The purpose of all art is to break the narrow boundaries of the finite, and open a window onto the infinite, for the benefit of the spirit of man, yearning in that direction."[3] It is certainly true that the need to break through the narrow boundaries of the finite finds its logical conclusion in complete freedom of expression, untrammeled even by the wish to imitate or produce resemblances.

From another standpoint, representational art is one of the most logical developments that art has seen for the last hundred years, the logic involved, of course, being that of creative life. However unexpected the varied manifestations of art have been in retrospect, they are seen to have been consistently moving away from representation. From Delacroix and Corot to Manet, then to the Impressionists, the Fauves, the Cubists, then to Paul Klee and so on, painters have progressively realized their power to infuse life into what Maurice Denis calls "a plane surface covered with colors, assembled in a certain order." As generations have gone by, objects have become less and less things that common sense sees and more and more paintings in themselves.

An artistic evolution is always complex, and it would be wrong to claim that every painter today would find it difficult to achieve a really good representational work. The contrary is proved by the good realist works that are being produced even now. We cannot trace any development into an unseen future, for we cannot possibly forecast what any

[3] Discourse to the congress of Catholic artists, September, 1950.

of the conditioning factors will be or what talents may emerge. But in the trend as we see it now, we can quite understand why many artists have lost the taste for the sort of work that was produced by their predecessors and are determinedly following the course on which they set out. Bazaine, Estève, Manessier, Singier, and Ubac began as representational painters, but they have all been forced to go beyond this stage.

The internal logic of this evolution is apparent in the growing awareness that artists are able to convey their inner world directly, whereas they had previously conveyed it by means of externals. This inner world is spiritual and sensual at the same time. It is *inner* in that it is within the universe and within the artist's soul. With Bazaine we can say that it is hidden in the external reality of things,[4] or we can say, like Manessier, that it envelops everything.[5] The validity of painting at all times has depended on the degree of inner existence which the artist has managed to give to reality.[6] The chief characteristic of the inner world for the artist is the pure rhythmic motif of *being*, over and above the figures that external objects offer to the senses. The pure motifs are the things the artist "abstracts." The degree of *abstraction* in a painting can be grasped only in relation to these motifs, and it is much more important to discern the degree to which the work of art *resembles* the inner world

[4] Jean Bazaine, *Notes sur la Peinture d'Aujourd'hui* (Paris: Fleury, 1948), pp. 49 ff.

[5] Hartung, in "*Pour ou contre l'Art abstrait*," *Cahiers des Amis de l'Art*, no. 11 (1947), p. 50.

[6] An article by Bazaine in *Le Figaro*, December 30, 1944.

than to establish the degree of representational literalism or nonrepresentational freedom. Thus Bazaine formulated the paradox, "Zola is less imitative (less abstract) than Mallarmé, Cormon is less imitative (less abstract) than Klee, and Klee is less imitative (less abstract) than the Douanier Rousseau. Kandinsky is much less abstract than Breughel or Vermeer, while Vermeer is the most abstract painter of all."[7]

It was obvious that a time would come when the artist would realize that his inner world was enough. Painting and sculpture have followed Mallarmé: "I have begun my *Hérodiade* at last; I find it terrifying because I am inventing a language which must necessarily take its rise from a completely new idea of poetry. Instead of trying to paint the thing, I am trying to paint the effect it produces." He is speaking of a psychological effect. "My verse, then, must be composed of meanings rather than words."[8] In 1891 Mallarmé told a journalist, "If you name the object, you cut out three-quarters of the enjoyment of the poem. By enjoyment I mean guessing at what is meant, little by little. All I want to do is *suggest*." Whether or not the object is recognized is beside the point, as long as the perceptible and spiritual qualities that correspond to it are expressed.

In painting and sculpture, mass and color and rhythm have the power to suggest. The "pure rhythmic motifs" that beings hold for the artist have a correspondence (in the creator and in the audience) to "physical reflexes, impulses,

[7] Bazaine, *Notes . . .* , pp. 49 ff.
[8] Letter from Mallarmé to Cazalis, dated October, 1864, in Mondor, *Vie de Mallarmé*, p. 145.

desires, sensations, and conceptions of the world."[9] Art has always been based on this correspondence, abstracted from the appearance of things. It has always broken away from "the crude myth that reality is something completely defined, delineated, and dead" in order to raise us up to its own level, giving us a share in the spiritual vision of the world. The esthetic experience is not something that makes us suddenly feel that we have our feet firmly planted on the ground; quite the contrary, it is a sensation of losing our footing and being uplifted. Thus Manessier could write, "Our task is to reveal, by genuine plastic means, the spiritual correspondence between outer and inner worlds, and to make this correspondence intelligible by the transpositions that art can effect."

This being so, it is obvious that the representation of appearances means nothing to the artist in comparison with the importance of winning back the prized inner dimension, the spiritual substance, which has been dissipated and ruined by slavish representation and superficial empiricism in art. On the other hand, the artist must not lose contact with the perceptible world. Bazaine said that "If we refuse all contact with the external world, we are committing suicide." Man cannot and must not try to emancipate himself from his incarnate condition, which stipulates that he cannot know anything he has not sensed. *Nihil est in intellectu quod prius non fuisset in sensu.* However abstract the process of his art may be, it can only achieve its purpose fully if it continuously returns to the perceptible world as the source of its inspiration. His work may eventually achieve

[9] This quotation and those that follow are from Bazaine.

the very perfection of harmony in the nonrepresentational manner, but it will be the harmony of the perceptible world which his art has transposed. Here we disagree with Hartung, who maintains that the artist is only making a detour if he expresses himself by going back to nature.[10]

Nonrepresentational artists who claim to be creating pure painting and pure sculpture completely apart from the perceptible world tend to become more sterile as they progress, and the few human and perceptible qualities in their work remain only by accident. The word *abstraction* inevitably evokes an intellectual tendency, and this is always dangerous in nonrepresentational painting. It has always been there, and we can see it particularly in artists whose poetic interpretation of being has made its appeal to the mind rather than the heart, the imagination, or the senses; in this sense, some works can be said to be more abstract than others, certain Romanesque frescoes, for instance, some paintings of Piero della Francesca, or Raphael's "School of Athens." Representational art implies a constant turning toward nature, but even this has not kept some artists free of sterility, particularly in the more academic phases of painting. A *fortiori*, the abstracting mentality is more dangerous in nonrepresentational art. As Manessier remarked, we are looking for some plastic sign language that can embody at the same time our perceptible world, precisely as *felt*, and the spiritual world as the ultimate revelation.

Just as the inner world I have been speaking of is in nature, in the artist, and in his work all at the same time, likewise it is within the beholder of the work. He recognizes

[10] Hartung, *op. cit.*, p. 49.

it as his own when he contemplates a true work of art. "When we look at representational painting," says Bazaine "the thing that appeals to us, seeming to recall past memories of our own, is not just a crude reality. It is not a state of things already existing but what we can ourselves create out of it by pure contemplation." It is sad that these words, which express so deep a truth and explain the question so perfectly, should explain at the same time why nonrepresentational art will never be popular. A crude reality is all that painting recalls for most people—either that, or feelings or ideas or yearnings that are so connected with the appearances that the artist offers in his picture as to be entirely dependent on them. Without them, most people's imagination has nothing to work on—at least at first glance, and probably for quite a long time afterwards.

One has to be equally aware of the limitations of abstract art, from the point of view this time not of its reception by the public but of the pictures themselves. Take, for instance, Tintoretto's "Paradise" in the palace of the Doges. When you look at it, you are not concerned with the figures in the composition except for Christ and the Virgin. This is typical of Tintoretto's paintings, of course. The faces are quite uninteresting as faces, while the figures themselves are lost in the great rhythmic waves of the total composition. These vast movements, made up of many figures, all in the same magical green tonality, are the only things that matter. One is always struck by the similarity of this heavenly host to the crowd of viewers in the hall where it hangs. What we are given is an enormous abstract decor. But we must remember that the picture carries its vast impression because of the representation of the figures. All the figures are as individual as each member of the crowd in the great hall beneath, which is why they both resemble and move the crowd. The forms, which one can certainly call abstract, are intensely alive, precisely because representational qualities are present throughout. If we were looking at mere colored curves, the impression of life would be nonexistent. The same is true of all the thousands of individual figures which we completely overlook in the windows and arches of Chartres.

If from considering this problem we turn to look at the extremely realistic paintings of Beaugin or Stoskopf, which are complex, subtle, and full of magic, we find that their enchantment is of a kind we would not experience from the sight of their pure lines alone or the objects they represent. I am thinking of Beaugin's little picture that shows a glass containing some pink liquid, a jug, and a plate of small cakes on a blue cloth, and of Stoskopf's little basket of blue glasses. They are so delightful that when we look at these paintings we can see the particular power of representational art at its best. They are so good that it is obviously not our sensory perception alone, delighting in the representation of familiar objects, that explains our enjoyment. Nature as well as the human spirit is fundamental to all our enchantment in the experience of works of art. We cannot heighten the power of nature except by immersing ourselves in nature. It is not enough to "abstract" ourselves from nature.

At the same time we must remember that each period in art can only be productive in the precise way in which artists perceive the correspondence between the forms of nature and those of man's inner world. In our period it would not be right to expect artists to give us what Beaugin and Stoskopf gave us, or even what Tintoretto gave us.

There is a depth and a seriousness in nonrepresentational art today that make it the obvious medium for religious painting and sculpture. This is certainly not because the nonobjective appeals to some Manichean inclination to suppress the material world, nor does it mean that we are aiming above the nature of man and trying to achieve some impossibly angelic ideal. There is nothing in it that is not consonant with faith. It does not imply a preference for the vague and a rejection of the hard, clear-cut lines of the Catholic creed. It does not imply false mysticism.

Most Christian artists in the nonrepresentational camp would agree with me in principle, I imagine, when I maintain that the art form that best corresponds to the order of the Incarnation must be the one that most clearly reveals the divine life of Word and Spirit in treatments that offer something familiar and recognizable. But it is a fact that the chief inspiration for many painters of today is rather the note that the Christian mysteries strike in the contemplative soul. They do not despise the different artistic treatments that these mysteries have been given during the long history of Christian painting and sculpture. They examine them minutely, precisely in order to get at what is most deeply hidden in Christian truths. Scripture itself is extraordinarily sober and reticent in the way it describes the external aspect of these things. The contemplative artist of today belongs to the current movement in which we are all being drawn into the depths of our own souls. In these depths, the artist finds his mysterious equation between inner and outer worlds, the world of the Christian mysteries, and their equivalents in painting and sculpture.

This obviously would not apply to the sort of nonrepresentational painting which sets out to produce nothing but the interplay of forms and colors. I am thinking only of the sort of abstract art that springs from the inner world and expresses it in a work of art. This latter sort of abstraction is admittedly unable to perform the task of explicit teaching, which is one of the most important functions of art in the Church. The principal purpose of this abstract art in churches will be to create an atmosphere conducive to contemplation, and by doing this it will help remedy the great danger of representational art, which may make us stop short at the mere external appearance involved in the mysteries and thus encourage a too superficial devotion that can border on the superstitious and idolatrous.

Whatever we may think about certain nonrepresentational works, it would be wrong to dismiss the whole art form out of hand. As it happens, we must face the fact that some of the best artists of our time (and they are among the most devoted children of the Church) are giving us of their very best when they produce abstract painting and sculpture. What I have tried to stress here is that they have become involved in this art form because that was the way their development lay. They had no option. What is sacred can only be attained in the depths of our souls, and the sort of art produced at this level is bound to show some detachment from what is transitory and perishable.

12

Church Architecture of Today

It is often argued that the functional quality of modern architecture is materialistic of its very nature. On the face of it this might seem to be the case, since it is influenced by two factors of the material order. The design is governed in the first place by the practical necessities of the people who are going to use it, and in the second place by the nature of the materials and building methods chosen. But it is important to remember that architectural forms cannot of themselves be considered materialistic any more than they can be considered pagan or Christian. They can be beautiful or ugly, logical or illogical, pure or debased, but nothing more. It is quite possible that some anti-Christian feeling may creep into purely functional architecture, but there is no reason at all why a Christian feeling cannot do the same. We have only to call to mind our great basilicas of Christian antiquity, which were originally palaces and baths—buildings not only thoroughly profane but connoting the most disedifying behavior. If in our time we feel unable to infuse a Christian spirit into architecture, that spirit must be very weak indeed.

It is not in the least necessary that religious architecture be different from the rest of the architecture of its period, as some people like to imagine. We must remember that every work of art has a particular significance, and if our churches give non-Christians the impression that we are no longer part of their society, we are encouraging a sectarian mentality and breaking up the essential communion of thought and feeling that should obtain throughout mankind. *"Terribilis est locus iste, vere domus Dei et porta coeli."*[1] A church is indeed a place of awe and wonderment, for it is God's house and the gate of heaven, as we are reminded on the feast of the dedication of a church. The Church must certainly express its separation from the world of sin and materialism, and this it does in the various laws laid down for the building of churches. But this means above all else that a church is a building designed for the celebration of the liturgy. This is its function and its whole purpose. It does not mean that the architect has to conform to any determined pattern of church building, and particularly so if it is not of his own period. He is a free creator, and his inspiration must not be stifled at the outset by any convention. Indeed, the systematized church architecture with which we are most familiar is for the most part only the result of prejudice. The architect must not employ an old, accepted form just because it is "traditional" in the mind of the general public. It is not sincere to do such a thing in our time. God cannot be honored today by something that belongs of its very essence to another period.

[1] Introit for the Mass of the Dedication of a Church; Gen. 28:17.

It is often maintained that people prefer to worship in a building that reminds them of the churches of old. And it is certainly true that the church is their house as well as God's and therefore must be built with their taste in mind. The reason people prefer churches in an earlier style, it has been suggested, is that they like to be taken out of their everyday atmosphere; and this is perfectly reasonable. If we accept this position, however, we are simply accepting the lamentable cleavage between the Church and the makers of art in our age. It is time we caught up with modern architecture and put it to the service of the Church, as was the case with architecture throughout our Christian past.

As far as the people are concerned, the initial impression of materialism that modern architecture made has already worn off now that we are familiar with so many buildings in the new idiom. The really good examples of modern church architecture are already being appreciated for their obvious excellence. What we have to do is help this valid art assume the position it must inevitably take, and above all we must not oppose it and hold the public back from appreciating it because of our own prejudices. The more modern churches we have, the more quickly public opinion will accept the idiom in which they are created.

The prescription of Canon Law dealing with the respect which architects who design churches owe to the hallowed forms that belong to our Christian heritage (Canon 1164, para. 1) is in no way violated by the splendid churches in which architects have been allowed to use modern techniques. To point out only a few, Notre Dame du Raincy

(Auguste Perret) opened the way in 1922, and in 1933 Fritz Metzger's Karlikirche in Lucerne; then came the churches at Dornach in 1942, St. Michael and All Saints' Churches in Basle by Hermann Baur, and Rouvière's Notre Dame de la Trinité in Blois in 1937. In each of these churches we find a perfect adaptation to the needs of the liturgy, true religious value, plastic beauty, an accord with tastes of the age, and a great variety of forms and expressions.

Here it may be profitable to consider what is the fundamental difficulty raised by modern methods in regard to church architecture. There is certainly a problem involved, which is often overlooked by traditionalists and modernists alike. For many of the latter, for instance, whatever is functional from the point of view of construction must necessarily be both beautiful and sacred. Some go so far as to claim that the only possible material that can be used is reinforced concrete, whereas, in fact, the primary question of economy will often justify the use of concrete for broad roof spans, for instance, and of the old materials—brick, stone, wood—in other parts. Economy must be a concern in architecture, as it must be for the mathematician who is always looking for the most concise solution to his problem. A beautiful form is always the most economical, and if the form is not beautiful, it means that true economy has not yet been achieved.[2] Nonetheless, the discovery of true economy demands, with modern techniques even more than old

[2] I thank the architect Le Caisne for this double formula.

ones, a rigorous spirit attuned to the harmony of forms in an almost musical sense. There must be a feeling for the necessary connection of these forms to their surroundings and, when it comes to building churches, a feeling for the sacred.

A purely technical study of the question can certainly lead us to magnificent forms. As we know very well, there are bridges and factories so splendidly designed that we have only to look at them to be inspired with an almost religious reverence for their hamony and proportion. Because of the general degeneracy of taste in our time, such works would probably have been ruined by any deliberate intention on the architect's part to produce something beautiful. But a church is usually considered as something more complex than a bridge, and so the technical economy of means which will be revealed in a beautiful form is not in fact revealed unless the architect's mind, while designing it, is awake to the purity of forms.

This has always been the case, but modern techniques, particularly the use of steel girders and reinforced concrete, make the need greater than it was in times past, precisely because these techniques give the impression that they can produce any required effect. This is an illusion, because concrete imposes more limits than it appears to, and it demands its own sincerity of construction. Its requirements must be very carefully studied and considered, not in the material order but rather in the moral order. It is precisely when everything is allowed that one has to lay down for one's own benefit an inner law, a certain discipline. What concrete demands above all, more than any other building material, is an equilibrium between structure and form, a knowledge of how the material will look when its proportions have been determined, and a knowledge of and adaptation to its limitations.[3]

Economy, understood too facilely, gives the most appalling vulgarity to concrete, more than to any other material. Le Caisne, explaining why we so often see uninteresting shapes in concrete, said that such ugliness only warns us that true economy has not yet been reached. We need more study of the question, investigating it as we would a dance figure. The analogy is surely perfect, since of its nature dancing is the most sacred of the arts, to the same degree to which it can become the most frivolous and sensual. Dancing is a dynamic architecture in which rigorous economy of movement in space attains, by a complete asceticism, a supreme ease and triumph of the spirit. And the guiding factor in the technical study which Le Caisne requires is a feeling for the quality of forms, which their capacity for causing us pleasure or pain. Beyond the impressions of our senses, there is the impression caused deeper down in our souls. Reinforced concrete pushes to the extreme the universal experience that technique comprises internal demands which have to be understood and for which a certain spirit is required. One is reminded of the German proverb, "The fineness of the materials is greater than the fineness of men." But it is for the human spirit to bring out this fineness. Without spiritual perception, mere technique is the most dangerous thing in the world.

[3] A. Hermant, in *Techniques et Architecture*, January, 1944, p. 5.

Of Our Lord's beatitudes recorded by St. Matthew,[4] there are four which have an immediate reference to architecture. There is poverty, for instance, seen as detachment from the material instead of subjection to and seduction by the material; this is a feeling for the divine transcendence in regard to which all creatures are called upon to rid themselves of pretension. Then there is the hunger and thirst for justice, which means, in architecture, the demand for absolute justice in the disposal of means. Purity is the refusal of all vain complacency, bias, compromise, and baseness. Peace is the final and supreme reward of architectural wisdom. It will shine out from the quality of forms elaborated by a mind and a spirit in which harmony reigns. When the architect works in this spirit, how absurd systems must seem, and how free he will be in regard to modern techniques.

A sensitive architect will use all kinds of materials, because he will love their individual qualities. He will employ forms which have been used in the past if they happen to come to him naturally; he may observe some eternal quality more perfectly illustrated in an earlier period, and when he adopts it for his own work, it will be bound to give out an *air de famille* with works of the past. But this is perfectly legitimate. It is in fact the best way to be traditional, that is, inwardly traditional because one is faithful to the abiding qualities of one's art.

Some forms will always seem to be particularly alive in certain places where they belong—the pepperpot church

[4] Matt. 5:3–11.

towers of Austria, for instance. It would be just as silly to proscribe such forms as these as it is to proscribe the most modern forms. But it would be equally foolish to insist on producing a work with regional characteristics just for the sake of being local. One cannot lay down either uniformity or diversity as a postulate anywhere. There was a great deal of uniformity in the pre-Romanesque from Ireland to Armenia, from Sweden to Syria, just as there is today in our modern style. A form of construction may be valid everywhere and be translated into similar forms in many places; it is equally likely that the influences of climate and the use of local materials will bring in regional variations. Once again we see the principle verified that the artist must work from within his own inner world and be faithful to the data he has to work with, the two aspects to be thoroughly integrated in himself.

All things considered, an objective judgment will surely acknowledge that there is much to be gained by employing the architectural resources of our time for the liturgical celebration of the community. The biggest problem in church building has always been that of the roof; but now this problem is solved, thanks to reinforced concrete. Arches, vaults, and girders nowadays have little weight in comparison with the monolithic arches of the past. And these means are put at the architect's disposal precisely at a time when the liturgical renaissance demands a thoroughly communal celebration. Such a celebration shows the architect what space is required, and however large it may be, there is no difficulty in enclosing it.

The types of buildings in which these new techniques have been used are necessarily various, but their common characteristic is lightness, delicacy. This is the most striking contrast between the churches of today and the vaulted stone churches of old.

However, one must be honest about the potential of reinforced concrete and admit that unless one submits it to some costly decorative process it usually remains cold and severe in appearance. Instead of disguising it, we can only hope to transcend it by concentrating on the beauty, the grace, and the nobility of the proportions which it allows us to achieve. There are great possibilities here for elegant rhythms and powerful and beautiful volume and mass, as well as for a more ingenious distribution of light and shadow that will favor recollection. Above all, there is the possibility of achieving an austere framework in which a few elements of particular importance can be made dominant.

There are many such churches, particularly in the German-speaking cantons of Switzerland, which are extremely striking because of their deeply spiritual character. They appeal to the imagination and to the heart. Some of them are incredibly lyrical—All Saints' in Basle, for instance, with its superb ranks of columns that make such a magnificent approach to its majestic sanctuary.

The spirit can be served, let us not forget, by the most exclusively industrial processes. There is not the least need to be suspicious of prefabrication, for instance. Otto Bartning has built about fifty small churches in Germany with prefabricated materials, but far from being conscious that they form a series, one is principally struck by the fact that each seems unique.[5]

The needs of the liturgy are thus perfectly satisfied, as are the needs of the community. The logic of construction and the expression of a feeling for the pure, the clear-cut, and the true are admirably satisfied by the architecture of today, though unfortunately not often enough. We have some examples of good church architecture, but hundreds and thousands of structures all over postwar Europe reveal only too clearly the confusion of our age. Christianity should be at its most vital in a time when dangerous currents have to be turned to the glory of God. But no one can truly consider modern architecture as a dangerous current. It has been branded as materialistic and therefore anti-Christian, but only by those who insist on condemning anything new on principle and whose reading of the Gospel is Pharisaical. Such reactionaries will certainly never triumph in the pagan world we in fact live in.

[5] See *L'Art Sacré*, December, 1950.

13

THE ACHIEVEMENTS OF OUR AGE

The churches of Assy, Vence, and Audincourt have made news. This was inevitable, owing to the celebrity of Bonnard, Rouault, Matisse, Braque, and Léger. Magazine articles, radio talks, movies, and even a certain amount of tourist traffic have added to the publicity. The Church has appealed to the great names in contemporary art, and the fact that these great masters have responded has become in itself an appeal to the world at large. Assy, Vence, and Audincourt have become symbols of the fact that great art is again possible in the Church. Signs of vigor have appeared after two hundred years of quiescence, signs that show unmistakably the freshest creative impulses allied to a feeling for what is eternally sacred.

Curiosity has been the reaction of some, snobbery of others, but there are many more who are deeply moved by these signs of our times. There are many people who are intensely concerned lest these signs be destroyed in the name of that very faith of which they are such a noble expression. It is one of the saddest things that can possibly happen when, inside or outside the Church, truly valuable works are ridiculed in the name of the Church itself.

The three churches in question, let it be understood, are not to be regarded as prototypes. They are simply worthy examples of the growing conviction that only the best will do for God's service. As Père Couturier has said, our duty is to bring to God and to our faith everything that is excellent in modern art. And the best of modern art obviously comes from the best modern artists—not the best known, or the most advanced, but those whom we can judge by their works to be the greatest and the most vital.

This is necessary for the honor of God and of the Church. It is also necessary for future generations, since the criterion of excellence is not fashion but creative value—poetic value, in the literal sense, which never decreases. Only the poets, as Victor Hugo remarked, possess the language that will speak to the future.[1] It is necessary, too, for the "little ones" whom Christ puts first. Many people think one ought to make an effort, stoop to a lower level, to please the "child-like," but in fact, by condescending to please, we demean them. It is high time that the dignity of the ordinary person, like that of the child, was treated with respect. It is worth taking the risk of alienating the smug and self-satisfied. In our age, when all is debased and degraded, anything of real genius, real beauty, is a stimulant that goes straight to the heart of the simple Christian and awakens an answering echo there.

The appeal to the masters of our time is a result of our

[1] Quoted in *Critique*, November, 1951, p. 956.

need for *genius*, by which word we understand *ingenium*, inventive power. Art lives by its living masters; the dead master, however valued, cannot give this lift to art. Only real genius can bring about the resurrection that art needs. We must go to whoever has the greatest talent, to the one who would seem to be best equipped to treat this or that theme, to perform this or that function. But nothing can be achieved without an acceptance of limitations, and so the artist has to realize what is within his capacity and accept his place in any artistic program.

Above all, we must give genius our confidence and our friendship. Normally, it must be admitted, the artist rarely receives these to the degree that he needs them. He is usually treated with suspicion, at least until such time as he is counted as a "Christian artist" because of his religious convictions. True friendship and trust between the artist and the priest commissioning his work are essential conditions for the success of the work. True friendship being wholly disinterested, its influence on the art work will also be disinterested. The friendship must be uncalculating—a true relationship and a mutual discovery. It is for the artist to discover or deepen in men the living realities of the faith on which their good works must feed; it is for the priest to see the values of art incarnated in the artist. It is vastly important for all artists, and not only for Catholic artists, to know that they are respected and esteemed by the clergy.

Think what wonders we might have in our churches today if Daumier, Van Gogh, Cézanne, Gauguin, Seurat, Degas, Manet, Rodin, and Maillol had been trusted and respected by the clergy of their time! But in fact there was

not a single French prelate in the nineteenth century who
was not either scornful or downright indignant about whatever works by these artists he knew. Can one imagine any
priest of that time discussing painting with Gauguin and
Cézanne, let alone asking them to consider painting for a
church? Even the harmless Puvis de Chavannes was considered "advanced"! One is intrigued by the fact that the
Abbé Hurel, who wrote a dull book on the Christian art of
his time in 1868, had at least some connection with Manet,
since Manet painted his portrait. But their dealings with
one another were sporadic and quite fruitless. What we
must have now is a real collaboration between clergy and
artists, with a view to the creation of genuine works of
sacred art.

A fruitful relationship between the priests and the artistic
creators of any one era is a sure criterion of the authenticity
of the forms that the life of the Church is taking at the
time. And when I say this I am not thinking of brilliant
salon conversations between distinguished prelates and celebrated artists. Obviously the Church's mission is not on
the order of merely human culture. What I am thinking of
is the mentality that we find common to the saints and
the simplest of people, which is on the level of genius. It is
not impossible to visualize a deeply satisfactory discussion
between some country priest who knows nothing about
"modern art" and one of the really good nonrepresentational artists of our time; they could understand each other
by means of their mutual understanding of souls and land-
scapes. It is not a question of artistic initiation and discussion as such, but of the mutual discovery of an inner world

—a mutual acceptance, recognition, and respect—of the sort which took place between Matisse and the bishop of Nice. This may not perhaps have been on the level of St. Anthony's visit to St. Paul the Hermit, but even so, it was on a certain spiritual plane where there was communion. I always wonder why Père Lacordaire in the nineteenth century had only the two Flemings, Janmot, and Cabat, good men that they were, for his artistic collaborators, and why Daumier, Delacroix, and Corot had no churchman with whom they might discuss their inner world. And by discussion I mean real down-to-earth talk, and not only an exchange of ideas. Why was it that Cézanne was unable to find a priest to touch the inner regions that he revealed in the words quoted in Chapter 1, "See the work of God!" But no priest, alas, would have given him a hearing with his odd ways and his "clumsy" painting.

Silence, poverty, a certain nobility, a feeling for the inner world—all these qualities were lost in the nineteenth-century Church as everywhere else. Holiness there was, and holiness can exist without these other qualities, but still it should be holiness that brings these things in her train when they are lacking. Fortunately, these qualities still managed to survive in the really great painters who were the heroes of art in their time. All this will give us some idea of what the friendship of the Church may do for the great artists of any period. Without it the artist is exiled from the realities of the spirit, while faith is busier denouncing errors than it is feeding on the life of God and spreading joy in the world. Art is suspect for the harm it may do instead of being accepted for its spiritual dimensions.

But it is time we left all this sterile mistrust behind and gave our friendship to the artist, who lives in a world through which, because it transcends appearances, the believer can understand what artistic creation means, while the artist for his part is empowered by his inner experience to reveal the riches of supernatural faith. Fortunately, the priest is not always so restricted by a formalized faith that he cannot allow himself to give the artist his full trust. The parish priests at Bréseux and Audincourt, the Mother General of the order to which Matisse offered his chapel, Canon Devémy, and Père Couturier have all given an unconditional welcome to artists on a scale perhaps not seen since the days of Tiepolo.

From the time of his training at the Ateliers d'Art Sacré under Denis and Desvallières, Père Couturier's greatest ambition was to revive Christian art by appealing to the independent masters of his time. He discussed the project many times between 1932 and 1935 with the Abbé Devémy, who was chaplain at a sanatorium in Assy, opposite Mont Blanc. In 1936, his friend Jean Hébert-Stevens, who worked in glass, spoke about the project to Bonnard, who was very interested; at this time, however, no opportunity came to make the work materialize. In 1938, Hébert-Stevens suggested to Père Couturier that he speak to Braque about his idea. The following year, in an exhibition of tapestries and stained glass which he organized at the Petit-Palais, Hébert-Stevens displayed several windows based on designs by Rouault. The Abbé Devémy was most impressed by these windows, and was given one, *"Le Christ aux Outrages,"* by

Rouault for the new church designed by Novarina which Devémy was building at Assy. Rouault was seventy at the time, and none of his works had ever appeared in a church.

Such were the modest and casual but significant beginnings of a great movement. Perhaps they were not, in fact, as casual as they appeared to be, since there was nothing casual about Père Couturier. On the other hand, he saw that there was no need to be systematic. The movement had to grow naturally. Each artist was to produce just what he felt like producing. During the German occupation, Devémy asked Bonnard to paint a picture of St. Francis de Sales to be put over the altar dedicated to him. Devémy had thought of Bonnard, with his extreme sensitivity to the beauty of the world, with his modesty and his consciousness of human wretchedness, as the very man to be attracted to St. Francis de Sales. Bonnard was at first amazed by Devémy's request, but then he began to read the works of St. Francis, and little by little he discovered the compassionate bishop for himself. And one can hardly imagine a picture more full of St. Francis's own particular kindness and graciousness.

After this, Rouault consented to having six of his pictures transferred under his own supervision to glass in order to produce the six low windows of the façade and of the mortuary chapel. Bazaine contributed three small windows in the choir which complement Rouault's work even though they belong to a completely different generation. For the altar it had been hoped that André Derain would paint a St. Dominic, but in the end it was Matisse who, while working on his chapel at Vence, offered a piece of enameled ceramic in yellow ocher on which the figure of the saint is outlined in simple strokes of black. The exceptionally large scale of the figure, the powerful freedom of its lines, and the simplicity of the material throw into relief the simple bronze tabernacle sculpted by Braque.

People come to Assy expecting to find a museum, and instead they receive the impact of the sacred. As soon as the church appears in sight, they are struck by Léger's mosaic, which covers almost the whole façade. Inside, the tapestry by Lurçat depicts with striking gravity the solemn drama in which every human soul is involved: The Beast strikes out at the woman of the Apocalypse, but is powerless against her deep assurance and serenity.

The central element of the ensemble was to have been Germaine Richier's crucifix, but owing to an antagonistic propaganda campaign based on an unfortunate photograph of the work, the bishop felt obliged to ask for its withdrawal. The photograph was admittedly rather a shock. It made the figure of Christ appear as an old, rotten bit of wood. In fact, when it was cast in bronze and actually in position in the church, it revealed its magnificently triumphal character. Possibly there was something at the same time too tragic about it for a liturgical ensemble, but the whole problem of the crucifix is, as we have already seen, to combine tragedy and glory, and the task is difficult. This crucifix certainly does combine the two ideas of supreme voluntary offering and the infamy of the gibbet. Christ is so identified in this work with these two aspects that I have to say I have never seen such a strong suggestion in art of the mystery of the cross.

The inevitable criticism Assy evoked did not come from the parishioners; on the contrary, the parishioners petitioned to have the crucifix back after it had been removed as unsuitable. It was unfortunate that the population of Assy should be mostly transients (mainly hospital patients), but insofar as it was possible, the parishioners of Assy were genuinely associated with the whole development of the church. The more understanding were immediately captivated by the idea, because they were made completely conscious of the religious value implied in the works and of their sacred function.

This was perhaps the most significant lesson learned at Assy. Until then, it had been taken for granted that really living works of art could never again be the expression of the religious life of the faithful, whether as individuals or as a community. The modern idiom, it had been assumed, was too shocking for the average parishioner, and it was feared that in his reaction against it he might also reject the religious truths embodied in such a language. But at Assy the fervor of parish life and the quality of prayer, whether of individuals paying their silent visits to the Blessed Sacrament or of the faithful during Sunday mass, signified a deep spiritual communion between the devotion of the faithful and the sincerity of the artists. It was the experience of this communion that eventually disposed of all prejudice and misunderstanding, and allowed the religious value of the works to make acceptable what otherwise would have been a *tour de force.*

As soon as one has true religious value and true plastic qualities in a work of art, then, with a little tact and a great

deal of love, its liturgical role allows the artist to break
through the barriers of incomprehension which normally
imprison him. Art is raised to its highest significance, exalting all that is best in mankind. The artist is no longer painting for the public but for the faithful. He is creating not
only a work of art but a sacred work. It is perfectly reasonable, although at the time it may have been unexpected,
that the Church should have granted Bonnard and Rouault,
Matisse, Léger, Bazaine the supreme achievement that
could only come to them in the house of God. Not the
state, nor generous patrons, nor political parties, but only
the Church can give the artist the opportunity for his full-
est expression for it is not until he works for the Church
that the artist is required to bring himself to a degree of
communion beyond the actual work, beyond himself as a
creator, and beyond those who behold the work and have
been helped by it to become contemplatives.

Gradually Matisse began to feel the inner necessity to
transcend himself in this way. Starting with a desire to
create windows, he was led, by the vision of a space alive
with colored light from these windows, to design a whole
chapel at Vence, the crown of his life's work. Père Couturier wrote, "He could not find the limitless spaces, the
infinite distances that he was seeking except in a building
itself open to spiritual space where man's life is no longer
bound by limits of either space or time."[2] For three and a
half years he worked on the project. His aim, he said, was
to create what he called "religious space," by which he

[2] Père Couturier, in *L'Art Sacré*, July, 1951, pp. 15–16.

meant a building of small proportions, to which he could give infinite dimension by the play of line and color. He wanted to create a place where people would come and feel themselves purified and lightened of their burdens.

To quote again from Père Couturier, "Matisse has never produced anything he did not feel from the beginning, completely, body and soul. He always identifies himself with the object he is painting, expressing it, as it were, in a single spontaneous flourish. As he said himself, 'Whatever I paint has to come from inside me, like a growing plant . . . and there comes a time when it is no longer myself, but a revelation. It simply comes out!' "[3] There is hardly any need to add that this is the outlook on artistic creation which should direct all religious art.

During the long period in which he was preparing himself for the moment of identification with the object to be painted, Matisse studied the artistic traditions and teachings of the Church, and became familiar with the life of the nuns who would be using the chapel. The result is a marvel for anyone who is not too conditioned by past experiences. The worldly become impatient, of course, when they see what Matisse has done, for it seems to them that he spent a great deal of time to no purpose. They see only a calculated return to the art of the cavemen, which ignores the whole development of art. In fact, Matisse's style is his own; and yet he was the first to be surprised by what he had produced, as I have commented before.

At Vence, the most controversial thing in the whole design is his treatment of the stations of the cross, which

[3] *Ibid.*

Père Couturier has described as "a page of barely legible writing, written under great stress, before which, even before we have read it, we know already the burden of what it has to say." The brush strokes tremble and break, then become heavy and disappear. The whole composition is full of movements of contradiction, seeming finally to fall to pieces under the sheer weight of the cross.

During the time Matisse was working on the designs for Vence, Manessier was also at work on church windows, this time for a little peasant church in Bréseux in the Jura Mountains. Manessier spent eighteen months on six windows, and he would have liked to have produced six saints, but an artist is not always allowed to do what he wants. In the windows he put all his love for the eucharist, magnifying the altar in a bright composition that was completely at home in its surroundings of fields and trees. The parishioners were at first disappointed when their saints did not materialize in the windows, but when they realized what Manessier had produced in place of the saints, they had no further regrets; they expressed the feeling that if they had had saints, they would have gotten used to them, but the windows Manessier made were different every time you looked at them. The windows are pure rhythms, pure harmonies, with the artist's whole heart and sensibility in them.

It was a striking tribute to the creator of the windows when the parish decided that the clutter of ornaments that was already in the church would have to go—even the war memorial of 1918 of which they had once been so proud! Here is a work that does in fact fulfill the Holy Father's plea for a reflection of divine beauty and light to smile on this earth and on our humanity, helping mankind to love all that is true and pure and good.

The experience at Bréseux was repeated, even more strikingly, at Audincourt. Père Couturier, asked to recommend some artists to decorate the new church there, approached Fernand Léger with a request for seventy meters of continuous windows circling the building just beneath the ceiling. He asked Jean Bazaine for a large mosaic for the façade. Léger and Bazaine made their designs, and these were offered to the working-class parishioners of Audincourt without any compromise. As Père Couturier said, "We respect you too much to make concessions to you." Léger and Bazaine became friendly with the people of the locality, and Bazaine wrote to me after his first visit there in most enthusiastic terms:

What an experience this has been! It has given me the answer to so many questions that have been torturing me—whether, for instance, I could express something definite and at the same time supernatural without using gimmicks or compromises; whether I could really make contact by this means with simple, down-to-earth people, the only ones, I find more and more, I really want to work for. There is no point nowadays in being an ivory tower or a voice crying in the wilderness. One has simply got to make contact, and find some usefulness for oneself in other people's lives. . . .

The people at Audincourt have accepted us completely. Audincourt itself is at the ends of the earth; there is nothing here at all, not so much as a stone. One has to begin from the beginning, but at least there will be a church now, so that a community can be built around it. I think people will find more life now, and more warmth.

This is the spirit in which the great works of our time are created. The church is dedicated to the Sacred Heart, and Bazaine's mosaic links a theme of water with one of sun and blood. The two inscriptions in the church are sufficient commentary: they are the words of St. Margaret Mary, "Jesus Christ appeared to me, blazing with glory, his five wounds shining like five suns," and the quotation from Isaias 12:3, "You shall draw waters with joy out of the Savior's fountains." Speaking of his mosaic, Bazaine has said he hoped it would appeal to people as something vigorous and joyful, like a river in summertime, and that it would not so much induce a mood of recollection, as make one wish to plunge into the church.[4] Inside the church, there are Léger's windows, made of thick slabs of glass set in concrete, celebrating the instruments of the passion. The central window depicts the Sacred Heart and the five wounds. There is something magnificent and at the same time restrained in all the forms Léger used here, and something truly sacred.

Audincourt is a very important step forward because of the unity and discipline with which the windows and the mosaic were elaborated, the immediate sense of a break with the profane world which they give, and the depth of spiritual communion they inspire among those who worship there.

[4] Jean Bazaine, in L'Art Sacré, November, 1951, p. 26.

14

The Task Before Us

There are many people, of course, who admit that it is a
splendid thing for the Church to employ famous artists, but
nevertheless feel that the results are barely tolerable. Even
well-disposed people often find it difficult to take artistic
creation seriously. At the back of their minds they always
have the conviction that the more extreme the artist is, the
less understandable his work is going to be to the general
public; the more independent and daring he is artistically,
the less suitable his work will be for a religious purpose.
Therefore, artistic independence must be tempered with
compromise.

Because there *is* opposition to modern art among the
faithful and the clergy, religious art must take its rise from
the life of these same faithful and clergy. Practically speaking, the majority of men cannot assimilate the art of today,
and therefore all one can do is consider not the general mass
of Christians but individual communities—the people and
the few priests who compose such and such a parish. The
fervor of Christian life in the community is the condition
sine qua non of artistic activity. There is no other way to

heed the warning of Pius XII that we must take into account the needs of the community rather than the personal taste and judgment of artists. Opposition between the community and the artist is disastrous, and compromise is no better. The only solution is to make the needs of a particular community play a really major part among the decisive influences that direct the inner activity of the artist. There must be friendship and mutual confidence between the artist and the priest, the priest as father and representative of the community. The artist's discovery of religion and the priest's discovery of art must both take place within the Christian community which is going to benefit by the eventual work of art so that all the faithful may share in the two experiences.

We may add that beautiful works mean little in a church if they are not signs of a humble Christian love. The inner world where the artist is deeply in communion with nature must reveal in the church its affinity with the truly Christian order. And that Christian order is embodied in those who live in Christ. Only humble, retiring love can justify our hopes for renewal, if, that is, this love can recognize the quality of the inner world into which it is led by genius. A little love can do more than the most zealous pharisaism.

First, we should single out certain tasks of immediate importance. One of these is the salvation of our old churches before they are finally lost to us. As Cardinal Suhard wrote,

The church is the noblest thing in any town or any village for all men, . . . be they Christians or unbelievers. *Noblesse oblige!* It is a nobility that demands that we be conscious of it. We must understand what the church meant to our fathers, and what it can still be and still mean to us. Such a nobility demands that we devote ourselves to its service; . . . this service will in turn ennoble us.[1]

Another valuable enterprise would be the multiplication of small churches or chapels. This demands large-scale organization and the sacrifice of many piously ambitious schemes and other interests that might seem to have priority. This is where we look to the prefabrication of churches, after the manner of Bartning, which I have already discussed. At the moment, this is perhaps too much to ask, but the need cannot be ignored.

At the same time, since it is normal that every age should leave behind its own special monument as an homage to God and as a pledge of its greatest possibilities, it would be an excellent thing if our age could leave behind something like the projected underground church of Le Corbusier at Sainte-Baume, or the basilica of St. Joan of Arc designed by Perret. In either of these cases, to speak for France alone, there would be the double sublimity of a great architectural conception and a gesture of the desire for peace and love on behalf of all our people.

Another really important undertaking would be the reforming of our cemeteries.[2] There was a time when the dead were buried very simply, with a common cross to com-

---

[1] Cardinal Suhard, in "Le Prêtre gardien d'un Patrimoine sacré," a pamphlet sent to all the French clergy in 1945, and printed in L'Art Sacré, nos. 3 and 4 (1947).

[2] See the article "Cimitières et Tombeaux," L'Art Sacré, November, 1940.

memorate them, not under incongruously pretentious monuments. There must be humility when our bodies are consigned to the earth if at no other time in our earthly careers. The place that signifies eternal rest was once a place with the most sacred character, but for many years it has been becoming more and more a place for clamorous ostentation and vulgarity. There is no distinction among the dead, so what can be the point of our trying to make distinctions for them? They are all awaiting the Last Judgment. But today, almost the only alternative to the cold necropolis of public cemeteries seems to be the appalling "garden of remembrance," the purpose of which is to make us forget death and along with it divine love.

There may not be much that we can do at the moment, but if the little we can do inspires in us a taste for the beatitudes of the Gospel, who knows what unexpected things may happen? To do what is possible means that we are recognizing our limitations and humbly accepting them, but more importantly it means that we recognize what our great resources are. Man is born to surpass himself, and grace is able to bring us a life that is infinite. But humility must hold us back when we thoughtlessly aim to go beyond what love enables us to do as children of God.

Before we can think in terms of art, we must realize that a humble love, not conventions and training, must underlie all evangelical and priestly work. All our activity must be bathed in love so that our liturgy, our preaching, our social contacts can bring back to all of us the fundamental ideal of Christian seriousness. This is the eternal value that divine love puts into everything in time; this is the dimension of the sacred.

If the Christian community is really animated by love, it will not be inclined to seek its expression in what is mawkish and sentimental. In one community the accent will be on missionary activity, in another on the liturgy, and in yet another on the works of mercy, but in every case the spiritual renewal of a community will be recognized and symbolized in whatever noble work is put into the church. If the priest has communed with the inner world of the artist, he will very likely pass on this experience to his flock. If the priest has welcomed into the church the artist who is to make it beautiful and noble, the people will do the same. They may be disturbed at first, but they will joyfully give the artist the same friendship and trust he receives from their priest. But a Christian community is only ready for mature and living works of art, of course, when the priest has disbanded that little circle of right-minded people who always think they know simply because they happen to have one or two unshakable theories.

Another proof of maturity on the part of the community is a real liturgical life shared by all. If this is present, then there must also be present, first, a taste for the highest activity possible to mankind—worship, and second, a feeling for inviolate spiritual values and for the joy that these produce. There must be a feeling for the sacred and a bringing together of all human activities penetrated by the divine in prayer, thanksgiving, praise, and sacrifice. As we know, even a sound understanding of the liturgy does not necessarily comprise a genuine idea of its artistic expression. Nonetheless, it does predispose people to a better understanding of what art should achieve, and it creates the atmosphere in which the faithful, their priests, and their artists can meet and so transcend their personal limitations that the ensuing art work is a manifestation of this transcendence.

This is the atmosphere in which the artist can acclimatize himself to the Christian outlook, educate his imagination in religion, and familiarize himself with the truths of faith by means of a living language of symbols. In this milieu, the artist can see how human life is lifted up to a higher level, changing the whole destiny of man. Only the liturgy can transform human anguish, in the individual and in the community, into the glory of God.

In the liturgy, truly lived and contemplated, an artist can find the realities that men live by in the Christian community. And the Church is then no longer in his eyes a mere administrative unit or a silent flock that obeys orders unreflectively. It is what it should be: his native element. He will not think of the faithful as his public, but rather he will see himself identified with them. And they in turn, in the measure that their liturgical education progresses, will recognize the artist's message as that of a prophet, speaking to them of the destiny of all men who are called to the peace and the glory of God.

I have already quoted Bazaine's letter from Audincourt. What a great joy it is for an artist when he finds the right atmosphere in which to work! It is a joy that makes him receptive to all the Christian virtues that are alive in the community. Christianity, as lived by sensible, down-to-earth, hard-working Christians, penetrates his whole being. He has no need to try to please the faithful, or to fear that his work will shock them.

A striking feature of Picasso's career is that at various times during his development he has produced portraits of exquisite delicacy, prompted either by love or by friendship. However violent the works he was engaged upon at the time may have been, these portraits have obviously been his spontaneous reaction to the people by whom he was most affected. The results have been pictures of touching simplicity. One can hardly believe, for instance, that the portrait of Madame Éluard in the Musée d'Art Moderne is later than "Guernica." These portraits represent some of Picasso's most decisive work, and one wonders if these are not the pictures that posterity will honor him for. At any rate, their nobility, charm, and deep intimacy make them truly great works, and surely the love of every artist for his fellow men in Christ and for their faith will bring about precisely this simplicity in his work. In the measure that an artist shares in the prayer of the children of God, to that measure will his brethren furnish him with precisely those means of expression in which they will recognize themselves.

In this way, art will be restored to the faithful. They will then discover that art is an activity, a mode of being, a gesture, an expression, a free language. It is all these together. However severely antagonistic factions may have condemned the authentic works which are the fruit of real

252   POTENTIALS OF LIVING ART

friendship among the faithful, the priests, and the artists in
our churches today, those who are in a position to judge are
unanimous in agreeing that these works do even more good
than a mission. Can one say more than that? This atmosphere of friendship is the climate in which it will be possible (perhaps even relatively easy, who knows?) to undertake the work that the future holds for us, and which I have
tried to sketch, after some years of reflection, in these pages.